The Power of the B1s

Gorton-built Thompson Class B1 4-6-0 No. 61344 drifts into Fort William station piloting Gresley Class K2/2 2-6-0 No. 61791 *Loch Laggan*. The pair head the 'down' express from Glasgow Queen Street and the South. Loch Linnhe laps the stonework outside the station and the hills beyond back Loch Eil and the Mallaig Extension. The three roads seen are the sum total of facilities at this terminus, while the goods sidings and motive power depot are way beyond signals in the background, right. 22nd June 1951.

E. D. Bruton

The Power of the B1s

Peter Swinger

OPC

Oxford Publishing Co.

Frontispiece: On 23rd June 1951 a fairly grimy No. 61341 from St Margarets Motive Power Depot (64A) heads north down the former Caledonian Railway main line from Stirling station with a late afternoon parcels train, which is probably bound for Dundee and Aberdeen via Perth. A hidden tank vehicle is the cause of the apparent gap between the locomotive and the van. The former North British Railway yard is seen in the far left.

E. D. Bruton

Title page: No. 61333 in almost spotless apple green livery and still retaining the bufferbeam number, rounds the curve just south of Hatfield with the 'up' 9.27am "Buffet Car Express" from Cambridge, with the stock in unchanged LNER teak livery and original style headboards. It is 16th April 1949 and the speed was logged at 55 mph. These trains were known irreverently to the undergraduates of the varsity city as the "beer trains".

E. D. Bruton

A catalogue record for this book is available from the British Library.

ISBN 0-86093-445-4

Published by Oxford Publishing Co.,
an imprint of Haynes Publishing,
Sparkford, near Yeovil, Somerset, BA22 7JJ

Printed in Great Britain by Butler & Tanner Ltd, Frome and London
Typset in Times Roman Medium

Acknowledgements

I record with gratitude my thanks to the following gentlemen for the use of their photographs: E. D. Bruton, H. Davies, A. R. J. Frost, A. Garraway, A. R. Goult, Anthony V. Gregory, Philip J. Kelley, S. C. Nash, B. Reading, R. C. Riley, E. Drummond Reynolds, D. B. Swale and Geoff Wignall.

To John Edgington for once more allowing me access to the photographs in the archives of the National Railway Museum and for his own pictures; to Michael Harris for allowing me access to the Real Photographs collection and to the Locomotive Club of Great Britain for use of photographs from the Ken Nunn Collection. A particular word of thanks to H. N. James for checking the initial manuscript and making corrections and suggestions, and for his photographs. To my Publishers and Peter Nicholson for the initial suggestion and the pleasure of preparing the book. And finally to my wife, Kay, for once more putting up with all the pictures strewn around and f or translating the hieroglyphics which masquerade as my hand writing, and producing a typescript there from.

I have endeavoured not to use photographs which may be familiar to the reader; where a picture has been previously published it has been used because its subject matter is of considerable importance.

Peter W. Swinger
Stowmarket

Introduction

When Sir Nigel Gresley died in harness in 1941, he was succeeded to the position of Chief Mechanical Engineer of the London & North Eastern Railway by his deputy, Edward Thompson. Official photographs of the new CME give the impression of an austere and, perhaps, humourless man. He quickly instituted a policy of locomotive standardisation throughout the LNER, as a result of which he has borne the calumny of succeeding railway enthusiasts for what he did to his predecessor's work.

Had he not used the pioneer Pacific *Great Northern* as his first rebuild, and had he left the P2s untouched, he might have been more fondly remembered, for his own Pacifics were good engines, as were the locomotives with which we are here concerned – his Class B1 4-6-0s. This class, introduced in 1942 under war-time conditions and restrictions, eventually ran to a total of 410 locomotives, though there were never more than 409 in operation at any one time, following the early demise of No. 61057. This locomotive was built in April 1948 and withdrawn at just two years of age, in April 1950, following an accident in which it was so severely damaged as to be considered beyond economical repair.

The B1s were constructed by five different manufacturers: the first batch of ten locomotives being built by the LNER itself at Darlington Works against an order placed in 1942. Given that the country was still in the throes of that unpleasant affair with the little Austrian corporal, it is understandable that permission was only obtained to produce a mixed-traffic locomotive, which the new engines were.

No. 8301 was the first one delivered into traffic in December 1942, but it was June 1943 before the second appeared. The first ten were numbered 8301 to 8310, but from January/February 1946 the class was renumbered from 1000. Darlington was responsible for the construction of the first 40 B1s, the original batch being fitted with sanding gear for forward running only.

An order was then placed with the North British Locomotive Company Limited who built numbers 1040 to 1130 at its Queen's Park Works. Further orders were placed in January 1946 with Vulcan Foundry, who built Nos 1140 to 1189, and another with North British Locomotive whose second order commenced with No. 1190 and ran into Nationalisation, culminating with No. 61339. Numbers 1190 to 1287 were delivered bearing the LNER running numbers but the next locomotive to enter service bore the interim British Railways numbering system, which consisted of an 'E' prefix, before the LNER number, as E1288. This practice continued to No. E1303, when the Railway Executive had decided upon the numbering policy for all locomotives owned by British Railways, and had decreed that the numbers of all ex-LNER engines should be advanced by 60000; the next B1 thus becoming No. 61304.

In December 1947 Gorton Works was instructed to build ten more engines, which entered traffic as Nos 61340 to 61349 while Darlington built Nos 61350 to 61359 against an order placed in November 1947. September 1948 saw BR place a further order with North British Locomotive Co. Ltd who built Nos 61360 to 61399 and the final batch of ten, numbered 61400 to 61409, was built by British Railways, Darlington, thus being responsible for the construction of the first and the last of the class. The B1s had, therefore, been built over a period of a little under eight years, almost entirely without variation; there had been some differences in the tenders, but no mechanical changes were made. Following withdrawal from revenue-earning service a total of 16 B1s were passed into Departmental use as stationary or mobile boilers for carriage heating. The precise details of date of entry into service, withdrawal date, names and changes in numbering, will be found in the accompanying listings.

Within his new Standardisation plans for the engines of the LNER Edward Thompson decided that his new 4-6-0s should be classified as Type B, the remit of the new design being to replace all 4-6-0s "not covered by the 6ft 2in Pacifics, D11s, D49s and all heavy 4-4-0 engines, C1s and other passenger Atlantics, K2s, K3s, J39s, and J6s and other 0-6-0s at present subject to fairly high speeds". This was a challenging remit which the B1s achieved in practice. The engines were to have the diagram 100A boiler, standard cylinders based on the K2 and the large or small Group-Standard Tender, as required and 6ft 2in driving wheels. The first engine diagram appeared in November 1941 and the final one in mid-1942: the locomotives were built with the boilers pressed to 225lb per square inch compared with the original intention of 220lb and weighing 74 tons 2 cwts.

On 29th June, 1942 the Chief Draughtsman at Doncaster advised the Chief Mechanical Engineer that he intended to classify the new engines 'B10' and sought approval. Thompson's reply was that they were to be "just B Type", but by 27th April 1943 he had changed his mind and issued instructions that the new locomotives were to be Class B1 and that existing ex-Great Central Railway B1s were to be reclassified as B18.

The B1s were to be known as the 'Antelope' class. Of the total of 410 built only 59 were named – 40 of them after antelopes, 18 after directors of the LNER and one, *Mayflower* received its name some time after entering service, and was the only member of the class named after Nationalisation. Given the number of breeds of antelope which inhabit our planet and the African continent in particular, it is quite amazing that the naming committee of the LNER contrived to duplicate the name of two members of the class, for *Nyala* and *Inyala*, and *Wildebeeste* and *Gnu* are respectively, two names for the same animal. It is also rather more than surprising that only one member of the class was named after a native British deer. *Roedeer* was the name given to No. 1040 – the only member of the first batch built by North British to receive a name.

Almost from the time that the steam locomotive became a familiar sight in Great Britain railwaymen in general, enthusiasts and enginemen in particular, have had a propensity for applying nick-names to various classes of locomotive. Was it not, therefore, asking for trouble to choose the name which was applied to No. 1005? *Bongo* – it was a gift, and practically from the day that No. 1005 entered traffic the B1s were known to enthusiasts (and to give credit where it is due) loved as the "Bongos".

They were strong, competent locomotives which worked the length and breadth of the London & North Eastern Railway system and in British Railways' days throughout the Eastern and Scottish Regions; they were a familiar site on the London, Midland Region, strayed onto the Southern and even the Western Region. Much has been written over the years comparing the "Bongos" with Stanier's "Black 5" 4-6-0 of the LMS, and each has been shown in a more favourable light. This is no place to renew that argument, save to say that during the Locomotive Exchange of 1948, when the B1 and Class 5 were tested over the same routes, the scales came down more often in the favour of the LNER engine, even on ex-LMS territory.

Most of the class had a working life averaging 20 years. With the onset of 'modernisation' some had ludicrously short careers, the shortest (with the exception of No. 61057) being No. 61395 which emerged from North British in February 1952, only to be withdrawn in October 1962. The record for longevity goes to No. 1002/61002 *Impala*, which was erected at Darlington in September 1943 and withdrawn in June 1967, a little short of 24 years, but even that was hardly a full working life for a steam locomotive.

Of the 410 B1s constructed two have survived into preservation and both were built by the North British

Locomotive Company Limited under order number L.963 placed in January 1946. Whilst it is sad that a London & North Eastern Railway built example has not survived, it is, perhaps, fitting that those which have came from North British who built the lion's share of the class.

Both of the survivors are privately owned, No. 1264 (BR No. 61264) being the property of Thompson B1 Locomotive Limited, and No. 1306 (BR No. 61306) is owned by Mr Gerald Boden. The former was the only ex-LNER locomotive to go to Woodham's scrapyard in Barry, from whence purchase took place in 1974, the locomotive moving to Loughborough on the Great Central Railway in July 1976 where restoration is taking place. It is the owner's intention that No. 1264 will be rebuilt to BR's main line standards and work on the boiler and firebox have cost just on £60,000 so far. As these words are written restoration work continues on the locomotive's frames and valve gear. The cylinders have been overhauled, new piston valves fitted, pistons re-ringed, the coupling and connecting rods have been re-bushed and bearings re-metalled, along with new drain cocks and cylinder pressure relief valves. It is hoped that the boiler will be returned by mid-1994, with the aim of returning to steam 18 months thereafter. A B1 working again in East Anglia in 1996? Let us hope so.

By contrast, No. 1306 *Mayflower* has led a very nomadic existence in private ownership: the locomotive has already enjoyed a seven year stint on the main line, followed by ten years on the Great Central Railway, from whence she went to Hull and on to Wansford on the Nene Valley Railway. Here, a further rebuild is taking place at the time of writing, by Gerald Boden and just three helpers; the frames and tender are complete and the boiler work is half-way through. Upon completion the livery will be LNER apple green but it is unlikely that a main line certificate will be sought on this occasion. However, there is the possibility of two B1s double heading on a preserved line.

Summary of Edward Thompson's B1 class 4-6-0s for the London & North Eastern Railway and British Railways Eastern Region

Original LNER No.	1946 LNER No.	BR No. Re No.	Date	Builder	Works/ Builder's No.	Name	Date Built	Date Withdrawn
Ordered August 1942								
8301	1000 Feb 46	61000	May 48	LNER Darlington Works	-	Springbok	December 1942	March 1962
8302	1001 Jan 46	61001	Apr 48	LNER Darlington Works	1912	Eland	June 1943	September 1963
8303	1002 Jan 46	61002	Apr 48	LNER Darlington Works	1916	Impala	September 1943	June 1967
8304	1003 Jan 46	61003	Dec 48	LNER Darlington Works	1920	Gazelle	November 1943	December 1965
8305	1004 Mar 46	61004	Oct 48	LNER Darlington Works	1922	Oryx	December 1943	December 1963
8306	1005 Feb 46	61005	Mar 49	LNER Darlington Works	1925	Bongo	February 1944	September 1962
8307	1006 Jan 46	61006	Jan 49	LNER Darlington Works	1927	Blackbuck	March 1944	September 1963
8308	1007 Jan 46	61007	Jan 49	LNER Darlington Works	1928	Klipspringer	April 1944	February 1964
8309	1008 Jan 46	61008	May 48	LNER Darlington Works	1931	Kudu	April 1944	December 1966
8310	1009 Mar 46	61009	Apr 48	LNER Darlington Works	1934	Hartebeeste	June 1944	September 1962
Ordered May 1944								
	1010	61010	May 48	LNER Darlington Works	1990	Wildebeeste	November 1946	November 1965
	1011	61011	Apr 48	LNER Darlington Works	1991	Waterbuck	November 1946	November 1962
	1012	61012	Jun 48	LNER Darlington Works	1992	Puku	November 1946	June 1967
	1013	61013	May 48	LNER Darlington Works	1993	Topi	December 1946	December 1966
	1014	61014	Jun 48	LNER Darlington Works	1994	Oribi	December 1946	December 1966
	1015	61015	Sep 48	LNER Darlington Works	1995	Duiker	January 1947	November 1962
	1016	61016	Nov 48	LNER Darlington Works	1996	Inyala	January 1947	October 1965
	1017	61017	Nov 48	LNER Darlington Works	1997	Bushbuck	January 1947	November 1966
	1018	61018	Jan 49	LNER Darlington Works	1998	Gnu	February 1947	November 1965
	1019	61019	Jul 48	LNER Darlington Works	1999	Nilghai	February 1947	March 1967
	1020	61020	Jul 48	LNER Darlington Works	2000	Gemsbok	February 1947	November 1962
	1021	61021	Dec 48	LNER Darlington Works	2001	Reitbok	March 1947	June 1967
	1022	61022	Feb 49	LNER Darlington Works	2002	Sassaby	March 1947	November 1966
	1023	61023	Jul 48	LNER Darlington Works	2003	Hirola	April 1947	October 1965
	1024	61024	Dec 48	LNER Darlington Works	2004	Addax	April 1947	May 1966
	1025	61025	Dec 48	LNER Darlington Works	2005	Pallah	April 1947	December 1962
	1026	61026	Jan 49	LNER Darlington Works	2006	Ourebi	April 1947	February 1966
	1027	61027	May 49	LNER Darlington Works	2007	Madoqua	May 1947	September 1962
	1028	61028	Apr 49	LNER Darlington Works	2008	Umseke	May 1947	October 1962
	1029	61029	Sep 49	LNER Darlington Works	2009	Chamois	June 1947	December 1966
	1030	61030	Dec 49	LNER Darlington Works	2010	Nyala	June 1947	September 1967
	1031	61031	Dec 49	LNER Darlington Works	2011	Reedbuck	July 1947	November 1964
	1032	61032	Jan 50	LNER Darlington Works	2012	Stembok	August 1947	November 1966
	1033	61033	Jan 50	LNER Darlington Works	2013	Dibatag	August 1947	March 1963
	1034	61034	Aug 49	LNER Darlington Works	2014	Chiru	October 1947	December 1964
	1035	61035	May 49	LNER Darlington Works	2015	Pronghorn	October 1947	December 1966
	1036	61036	May 50	LNER Darlington Works	2016	Ralph Assheton	November 1947	September 1962
	1037	61037	Feb 50	LNER Darlington Works	2017	Jairou	November 1947	May 1964
	1038	61038	Nov 50	LNER Darlington Works	2018	Blacktail	December 1947	May 1964
	1039	61039	Dec 49	LNER Darlington Works	2019	Steinbok	December 1947	June 1965
Order Number L958 - August 1945								
	1040	61040	Jun 48	North British	25796	Roedeer	April 1946	July 1966
	1041	61041	Apr 48	North British	25797		April 1946	April 1964
	1042	61042	Jul 48	North British	25799		May 1946	April 1966
	1043	61043	Apr 48	North British	25800		May 1946	July 1962
	1044	61044	Apr 48	North British	25801		May 1946	March 1964
	1045	61045	Sep 48	North British	25802		May 1946	September 1962
	1046	61046	Nov 49	North British	25798		May 1946	April 1962
	1047	61047	Nov 48	North British	25803		June 1966	September 1962
	1048	61048	Apr 48	North British	25804		June 1946	September 1962
	1049	61049	Mar 48	North British	25805		June 1946	November 1965
	1050	61050	Aug 48	North British	25806		June 1946	February 1966
	1051	61051	Mar 50	North British	25807		June 1946	February 1966
	1052	61052	Mar 48	North British	25808		June 1946	September 1962
	1053	61053	Jul 48	North British	25809		June 1946	February 1963
	1054	61054	Apr 48	North British	25810		June 1946	September 1962
	1055	61055	Jun 49	North British	25811		July 1946	February 1962
	1056	61056	Aug 49	North British	25812		July 1946	April 1964
	1057	61057	Apr 48	North British	25813		July 1946	April 1950
	1058	61058	Sep 48	North British	25814		July 1946	February 1966
	1059	61059	Jun 48	North British	25815		July 1946	November 1963

Continued on page ten

Previous page: April 1946 saw the appearance of the first B1 built by the North British Locomotive Co. Ltd at its Queen's Park Works. Of all the B1s built by that company, it was the only one to bear the name of an antelope, although a further 16 were named after LNER directors, plus *Mayflower*. No. 1040 was named *Roedeer*, and is seen in lined shop grey in the North British works. There are a number of differences of livery between No. 1040 and the LNER built example. The Darlington built engine has its wheels painted grey entirely, whereas North British chose to paint the rims black with 'LNER' in full on the tender, with shaded white lettering and numbering. A further point of interest is the diamond shaped builder's plate: those on the Darlington built engine are oval (see page 16).

Mitchell Library, Glasgow

Continued from page seven

Original LNER No.	1946 LNER No.	BR No. Re No.	Date	Builder	Works/ Builder's No.	Name	Date Built	Date Withdrawn
	1060	61060	Apr 48	North British	25816		August 1946	September 1962
	1061	61061	May 49	North British	25817		August 1946	September 1965
	1062	61062	Jan 49	North British	25818		August 1946	August 1964
	1063	61063	Mar 48	North British	25819		August 1946	March 1962
	1064	61064	Oct 48	North British	25820		August 1946	October 1962
	1065	61065	Mar 48	North British	25821		August 1946	September 1964
	1066	61066	May 50	North British	25822		August 1946	September 1962
	1067	61067	Nov 48	North British	25823		August 1946	December 1962
	1068	61068	Oct 49	North British	25824		August 1946	June 1963
	1069	61069	May 48	North British	25825		August 1946	September 1963
	1070	61070	Mar 48	North British	25826		August 1946	August 1965
	1071	61071	Apr 48	North British	25827		August 1946	February 1963
	1072	61072	Jun 48	North British	25828		September 1946	May 1967
	1073	61073	Mar 49	North British	25829		September 1946	September 1963
	1074	61074	Mar 48	North British	25830		September 1946	September 1963
	1075	61075	May 48	North British	25831		September 1946	September 1963
	1076	61076	Mar 48	North British	25832		September 1946	September 1965
	1077	61077	May 48	North British	25833		September 1946	May 1962
	1078	61078	May 48	North British	25834		September 1946	October 1962
	1079	61079	Apr 48	North British	25835		September 1946	June 1962
	1080	61080	Aug 48	North British	25836		September 1946	March 1964
	1081	61081	Mar 48	North British	25837		October 1946	June 1964
	1082	61082	Sep 49	North British	25839		October 1946	December 1962
	1083	61083	Jul 48	North British	25838		October 1946	September 1963
	1084	61084	May 48	North British	25841		October 1946	June 1964
	1085	61085	Aug 48	North British	25842		October 1946	November 1961
	1086	61086	May 48	North British	25840		October 1946	December 1962
	1087	61087	Nov 48	North British	25843		October 1946	December 1965
	1088	61088	Sep 48	North British	25844		October 1946	September 1963
	1089	61089	Mar 48	North British	25845		October 1946	April 1966
	1090	61090	Dec 49	North British	25846		October 1946	September 1963
	1091	61091	Jan 49	North British	25847		October 1946	September 1962
	1092	61092	Oct 48	North British	25848		October 1946	February 1966
	1093	61093	Mar 49	North British	25849		November 1946	July 1965
	1094	61094	Apr 49	North British	25850		November 1946	June 1965
	1095	61095	Mar 49	North British	25851		November 1946	December 1963
	1096	61096	Jan 49	North British	25852		November 1946	September 1962
	1097	61097	Mar 49	North British	25853		November 1946	January 1965
	1098	61098	Aug 48	North British	25854		November 1946	July 1965
	1099	61099	Apr 49	North British	25855		November 1946	September 1966
	1100	61100	Aug 48	North British	25856		November 1946	November 1962
	1101	61101	Jun 48	North British	25857		November 1946	December 1966
	1102	61102	Jul 48	North British	25862		December 1946	April 1967
	1103	61103	Aug 48	North British	25863		December 1946	July 1966
	1104	61104	Dec 48	North British	25864		December 1946	April 1964
	1105	61105	Jul 49	North British	25858		December 1946	December 1964
	1106	61106	May 48	North British	25859		December 1946	November 1962
	1107	61107	Oct 48	North British	25861		December 1946	August 1965
	1108	61108	Aug 48	North British	25860		December 1946	December 1962
	1109	61109	Oct 48	North British	25865		December 1946	July 1964
	1110	61110	Dec 48	North British	25866		December 1946	October 1965
	1111	61111	Jun 48	North British	25867		December 1946	September 1962
	1112	61112	Oct 48	North British	25868		December 1946	December 1962
	1113	61113	May 48	North British	25869		December 1946	September 1963
	1114	61114	Jul 49	North British	25870		January 1947	September 1962
	1115	61115	Oct 48	North British	25871		January 1947	May 1967

Continued on next page

Continued from previous page

Original 1946 LNER No.	1946 LNER No.	BR No. Re No.	Date	Builder	Works/ Builder's No.	Name	Date Built	Date Withdrawn
	1116	61116	Jul 48	North British	25872		January 1947	July 1966
	1117	61117	Jun 48	North British	25873		January 1947	February 1964
	1118	61118	Aug 48	North British	25874		January 1947	July 1964
	1119	61119	Dec 48	North British	25875		January 1947	November 1963
	1120	61120	Oct 48	North British	25876		January 1947	January 1965
	1121	61121	Nov 48	North British	25877		January 1947	April 1966
	1122	61122	Apr 48	North British	25878		January 1947	November 1963
	1123	61123	Nov 48	North British	25879		January 1947	May 1967
	1124	61124	Oct 48	North British	25880		February 1947	September 1962
	1125	61125	Nov 48	North British	25881		February 1947	December 1963
	1126	61126	Sep 48	North British	25882		February 1947	September 1963
	1127	61127	Sep 48	North British	25883		February 1947	August 1965
	1128	61128	Aug 48	North British	25884		February 1947	December 1962
	1129	61129	Mar 49	North British	25885		February 1947	September 1965
	1130	61130	Oct 48	North British	25886		February 1947	September 1962
	1131	61131	Sep 48	North British	25887		February 1947	December 1966
	1132	61132	Aug 48	North British	25888		February 1947	September 1966
	1133	61133	Apr 48	North British	25889		February 1947	September 1966
	1134	61134	Apr 48	North British	25890		March 1947	October 1965
	1135	61135	Dec 48	North British	25891		March 1947	September 1963
	1136	61136	Sep 48	North British	25892		March 1947	October 1962
	1137	61137	Dec 48	North British	25893		March 1947	May 1962
	1138	61138	Dec 48	North British	25894		March 1947	January 1965
	1139	61139	Feb 49	North British	25895		April 1947	September 1962

Order Number 2333 - January 1946

Original 1946 LNER No.	1946 LNER No.	BR No. Re No.	Date	Builder	Works/ Builder's No.	Name	Date Built	Date Withdrawn
	1140	61140	Jan 49	Vulcan Foundry	5498		April 1947	December 1966
	1141	61141	Nov 48	Vulcan Foundry	5499		April 1947	July 1965
	1142	61142	Mar 49	Vulcan Foundry	5500		April 1947	September 1963
	1143	61143	Jan 49	Vulcan Foundry	5501		April 1947	February 1964
	1144	61144	Feb 49	Vulcan Foundry	5502		April 1947	April 1964
	1145	61145	Dec 48	Vulcan Foundry	5503		April 1947	January 1966
	1146	61146	Aug 48	Vulcan Foundry	5504		April 1947	March 1964
	1147	61147	Nov 48	Vulcan Foundry	5505		April 1947	December 1965
	1148	61148	Mar 49	Vulcan Foundry	5506		April 1947	September 1966
	1149	61149	Nov 48	Vulcan Foundry	5507		April 1947	September 1962
	1150	61150	Sep 48	Vulcan Foundry	5508		April 1947	September 1962
	1151	61151	Oct 48	Vulcan Foundry	5509		April 1947	September 1962
	1152	61152	Jan 49	Vulcan Foundry	5510		May 1947	April 1964
	1153	61153	Dec 48	Vulcan Foundry	5511		May 1947	January 1965
	1154	61154	Nov 48	Vulcan Foundry	5512		May 1947	September 1962
	1155	61155	Dec 48	Vulcan Foundry	5513		May 1947	March 1964
	1156	61156	Jan 49	Vulcan Foundry	5514		May 1947	November 1963
	1157	61157	Oct 48	Vulcan Foundry	5515		May 1947	August 1965
	1158	61158	Feb 49	Vulcan Foundry	5516		May 1947	April 1966
	1159	61159	Sep 48	Vulcan Foundry	5517		May 1947	September 1963
	1160	61160	May 49	Vulcan Foundry	5518		May 1947	September 1963
	1161	61161	Feb 49	Vulcan Foundry	5519		May 1947	December 1966
	1162	61162	Feb 49	Vulcan Foundry	5520		May 1947	December 1964
	1163	61163	May 48	Vulcan Foundry	5521		May 1947	September 1962
	1164	61164	Dec 48	Vulcan Foundry	5522		May 1947	September 1962
	1165	61165	Aug 49	Vulcan Foundry	5523		May 1947	September 1962
	1166	61166	Mar 49	Vulcan Foundry	5524		May 1947	September 1962
	1167	61167	May 49	Vulcan Foundry	5525		May 1947	December 1964
	1168	61168	May 49	Vulcan Foundry	5526		June 1947	October 1965
	1169	61169	May 48	Vulcan Foundry	5527		June 1947	December 1963
	1170	61170	Oct 49	Vulcan Foundry	5528		June 1947	July 1962
	1171	61171	Mar 49	Vulcan Foundry	5529		June 1947	December 1965
	1172	61172	Oct 48	Vulcan Foundry	5530		June 1947	December 1965
	1173	61173	May 49	Vulcan Foundry	5531		June 1947	January 1967
	1174	61174	Jul 49	Vulcan Foundry	5532		June 1947	December 1963
	1175	61175	Jan 49	Vulcan Foundry	5533		June 1947	December 1963
	1176	61176	Sep 49	Vulcan Foundry	5534		June 1947	November 1965
	1177	61177	Jun 49	Vulcan Foundry	5535		June 1947	September 1963
	1178	61178	Oct 49	Vulcan Foundry	5536		June 1947	February 1964
	1179	61179	Mar 49	Vulcan Foundry	5537		June 1947	January 1965
	1180	61180	Dec 48	Vulcan Foundry	5538		June 1947	May 1967

Continued on next page

Continued from previous page

Original LNER No.	1946 LNER No.	BR No. Re No.	Date	Builder	Works/ Builder's No.	Name	Date Built	Date Withdrawn
	1181	61181	Mar 49	Vulcan Foundry	5539		July 1947	November 1963
	1182	61182	May 49	Vulcan Foundry	5540		July 1947	September 1962
	1183	61183	Mar 49	Vulcan Foundry	5541		July 1947	July 1962
	1184	61184	Jan 49	Vulcan Foundry	5542		July 1947	December 1962
	1185	61185	Mar 49	Vulcan Foundry	5543		July 1947	October 1964
	1186	61186	Mar 49	Vulcan Foundry	5544		July 1947	November 1962
	1187	61187	Mar 49	Vulcan Foundry	5545		July 1947	September 1962
	1188	61188	Mar 49	Vulcan Foundry	5546		July 1947	November 1965
	1189	61189	Dec 49	Vulcan Foundry	5547	Sir William Gray	August 1947	May 1967

Order Number L 963 - January 1946

Original LNER No.	1946 LNER No.	BR No. Re No.	Date	Builder	Works/ Builder's No.	Name	Date Built	Date Withdrawn
	1190	61190	Mar 49	North British	26091		May 1947	June 1965
	1191	61191	Jun 49	North British	26092		May 1947	August 1965
	1192	61192	Apr 49	North British	26093		May 1947	October 1962
	1193	61193	Jan 49	North British	26094		May 1947	September 1962
	1194	61194	Feb 49	North British	26095		May 1947	August 1965
	1195	61195	Dec 48	North British	26096		May 1947	November 1965
	1196	61196	Aug 49	North British	26097		May 1947	September 1965
	1197	61197	Nov 48	North British	26098		May 1947	June 1964
	1198	61198	Oct 48	North British	26099		June 1947	April 1965
	1199	61199	May 48	North British	26100		June 1947	January 1967
	1200	61200	Jul 49	North British	26101		June 1947	December 1962
	1201	61201	Jul 49	North British	26102		June 1947	January 1962
	1202	61202	Mar 49	North British	26103		June 1947	September 1962
	1203	61203	Jun 49	North British	26104		June 1947	July 1962
	1204	61204	Aug 48	North British	26105		June 1947	November 1963
	1205	61205	Apr 49	North British	26106		June 1947	November 1963
	1206	61206	Nov 49	North British	26107		July 1947	September 1962
	1207	61207	Aug 49	North British	26108		June 1947	December 1963
	1208	61208	Nov 49	North British	26109		July 1947	September 1965
	1209	61209	Aug 49	North British	26110		July 1947	September 1962
	1210	61210	Sep 49	North British	26111		July 1947	February 1966
	1211	61211	May 49	North British	26112		July 1947	November 1962
	1212	61212	Jun 49	North British	26113		July 1947	November 1964
	1213	61213	Sep 49	North British	26114		July 1947	April 1964
	1214	61214	Apr 50	North British	26115		July 1947	May 1965
	1215	61215	Apr 49	North British	26116	William Henton Carver	July 1947	March 1965
	1216	61216	Mar 49	North British	26117		July 1947	January 1967
	1217	61217	Sep 48	North British	26118		August 1947	March 1962
	1218	61218	Nov 48	North British	26119		August 1947	May 1965
	1219	61219	Sep 48	North British	26120		August 1947	June 1964
	1220	61220	Jul 50	North British	26121		August 1947	October 1965
	1221	61221	Sep 49	North British	26122	Sir Alexander Erskine-Hill	August 1947	March 1965
	1222	61222	Sep 48	North British	26123		August 1947	January 1962
	1223	61223	Dec 49	North British	26124		August 1947	January 1966
	1224	61224	May 49	North British	26125		August 1947	July 1966
	1225	61225	Oct 49	North British	26126		August 1947	June 1965
	1226	61226	Apr 49	North British	26127		August 1947	September 1963
	1227	61227	Feb 50	North British	26128		August 1947	September 1963
	1228	61228	Oct 49	North British	26129		August 1947	September 1962
	1229	61229	Dec 49	North British	26130		September 1947	June 1964
	1230	61230	Oct 49	North British	26131		September 1947	November 1962
	1231	61231	Jan 50	North British	26132		September 1947	July 1962
	1232	61232	Aug 49	North British	26133		September 1947	February 1966
	1233	61233	Sep 47	North British	26134		September 1947	November 1963
	1234	61234	Apr 49	North British	26135		September 1947	August 1962
	1235	61235	May 49	North British	26136		September 1947	September 1962
	1236	61236	Feb 49	North British	26137		September 1947	September 1962
	1237	61237	Feb 49	North British	26138	Geoffrey H Kitson	September 1947	December 1966
	1238	61238	Jul 48	North British	26139	Leslie Runciman	September 1947	February 1967
	1239	61239	Dec 48	North British	26140		October 1947	August 1962
	1240	61240	Apr 49	North British	26141	Harry Hinchliffe	October 1947	December 1966
	1241	61241	Jul 48	North British	26142	Viscount Ridley	October 1947	December 1962
	1242	61242	Apr 49	North British	26143	Alexander Reith Gray	October 1947	July 1964
	1243	61243	Mar 49	North British	26144	Sir Harold Mitchell	October 1947	May 1964
	1244	61244	Apr 49	North British	26145	Strang Steel	October 1947	October 1965
	1245	61245	May 48	North British	26146	Murray of Elibank	October 1947	July 1965

Continued on next page

Continued from previous page

Original LNER No.	1946 LNER No.	BR No. Re No.	Date	Builder	Works/ Builder's No.	Name	Date Built	Date Withdrawn
	1246	61246	Nov 49	North British	26147	Lord Balfour of Burleigh	October 1947	December 1962
	1247	61247	Aug 49	North British	26148	Lord Burghley	October 1947	June 1962
	1248	61248	Jun 50	North British	26149	Geoffrey Gibbs	October 1947	November 1965
	1249	61249	Jun 50	North British	26150	Fitzherbert Wright	October 1947	June 1964
	1250	61250	Jun 50	North British	26151	A. Harold Bibby	October 1947	April 1966
	1251	61251	May 48	North British	26152	Oliver Bury	November 1947	April 1964
	1252	61252	Jun 49	North British	26153		November 1947	November 1963
	1253	61253	Jun 49	North British	26154		November 1947	September 1962
	1254	61254	May 49	North British	26155		November 1947	September 1962
	1255	61255	Nov 48	North British	26156		November 1947	June 1967
	1256	61256	Mar 49	North British	26157		November 1947	November 1965
	1257	61257	Apr 49	North British	26158		November 1947	October 1965
	1258	61258	Feb 49	North British	26159		November 1947	January 1964
	1259	61259	Jan 49	North British	26160		November 1947	August 1965
	1260	61260	Jun 49	North British	26161		November 1947	December 1962
	1261	61261	Jun 49	North British	26162		November 1962	September 1966
	1262	61262	Jun 49	North British	26163		December 1947	June 1967
	1263	61263	May 49	North British	26164		December 1947	December 1966
	1264	61264	Oct 49	North British	26165		December 1947	November 1965
	1265	61265	Jun 48	North British	26166		December 1947	February 1962
	1266	61266	May 48	North British	26167		December 1947	September 1962
	1267	61267	Jan 49	North British	26168		December 1947	December 1962
	1268	61268	May 50	North British	26169		December 1947	December 1964
	1269	61269	Dec 49	North British	26170		December 1947	December 1963
	1270	61270	Sep 49	North British	26171		December 1947	September 1963
	1271	61271	May 49	North British	26172		December 1947	July 1962
	1272	61272	Jul 49	North British	26173		December 1947	January 1965
	1273	61273	Mar 50	North British	26174		December 1947	May 1963
	1274	61274	Mar 50	North British	26175		January 1948	November 1964
	1275	61275	May 50	North British	26176		January 1948	October 1965
	1276	61276	May 50	North British	26177		January 1948	June 1965
	1277	61277	May 49	North British	26178		January 1948	June 1964
	1278	61278	Oct 49	North British	26179		January 1948	April 1967
	1279	61279	Oct 49	North British	26180		January 1948	September 1963
	1280	61280	Jan 50	North British	26181		January 1948	September 1962
	1281	61281	Dec 49	North British	26182		January 1948	February 1966
	1282	61282	Apr 49	North British	26183		January 1948	September 1962
	1283	61283	Nov 48	North British	26184		February 1948	September 1962
	1284	61284	Feb 50	North British	26185		February 1948	September 1962
	1285	61285	Mar 49	North British	26186		February 1948	December 1965
	1286	61286	Sep 49	North British	26187		February 1948	September 1962
	1287	61287	Jul 49	North British	26188		February 1948	September 1962
	E1288	61288	Jun 50	North British	26189		February 1948	January 1964
	E1289	61289	Nov 49	North British	26190		February 1948	June 1967
	E1290	61290	Aug 49	North British	26191		February 1948	March 1962
	E1291	61291	Jun 50	North British	26192		February 1948	May 1965
	E1292	61292	Jun 48	North British	26193		February 1948	September 1965
	E1293	61293	Dec 49	North British	26194		February 1948	August 1966
	E1294	61294	Nov 49	North British	26195		March 1948	November 1964
	E1295	61295	Jun 50	North British	26196		March 1948	November 1962
	E1296	61296	Jul 50	North British	26197		March 1948	November 1962
	E1297	61297	Mar 50	North British	26198		March 1948	November 1962
	E1298	61298	Oct 48	North British	26199		March 1948	June 1962
	E1299	61299	Dec 49	North British	26200		March 1948	July 1965
	E1300	61300	Jun 49	North British	26201		March 1948	November 1963
	E1301	61301	Dec 49	North British	26202		March 1948	September 1962
	E1302	61302	Aug 49	North British	26203		March 1948	June 1966
	E1303	61303	Aug 50	North British	26204		March 1948	November 1966
		61304		North British	26205		March 1948	October 1965
		61305		North British	26202		April 1948	October 1963
		61306		North British	26207		April 1948	September 1967
		61307		North British	26208		April 1948	November 1966
		61308		North British	26209		April 1948	November 1966
		61309		North British	26210		April 1948	January 1967
		61310		North British	26211		April 1948	April 1965
		61311		North British	26212		April 1948	September 1962
		61312		North British	26213		April 1948	March 1964

Continued on next page

Continued from previous page

Original LNER No.	1946 LNER No.	BR No. Re No.	Date	Builder	Works/ Builder's No.	Name	Date Built	Date Withdrawn
		61313		North British	26214		April 1948	November 1965
		61314		North British	26215		April 1948	December 1963
		61315		North British	26216		April 1948	February 1966
		61316		North British	26217		May 1948	December 1962
		61317		North British	26218		May 1948	September 1962
		61318		North British	26219		May 1948	September 1963
		61319		North British	26220		May 1948	December 1966
		61320		North British	26221		May 1948	August 1965
		61321		North British	26222		May 1948	August 1964
		61322		North British	26223		May 1948	February 1966
		61323		North British	26224		May 1948	November 1963
		61324		North British	26225		June 1948	October 1965
		61325		North British	26226		June 1948	September 1963
		61326		North British	26227		June 1948	March 1966
		61327		North British	26228		June 1948	February 1965
		61328		North British	26229		June 1948	September 1963
		61329		North British	26230		June 1948	April 1966
		61330		North British	26231		June 1948	November 1966
		61331		North British	26232		June 1948	September 1963
		61332		North British	26233		June 1948	December 1962
		61333		North British	26234		July 1948	December 1962
		61334		North British	26235		July 1948	December 1963
		61335		North British	26236		July 1948	September 1962
		61336		North British	26237		August 1948	September 1963
		61337		North British	26238		August 1948	September 1967
		61338		North British	26239		August 1948	January 1965
		61339		North British	26240		September 1948	November 1962

Ordered December 1947

		61340		BR Gorton Works	998		November 1948	April 1966
		61341		BR Gorton Works	999		December 1948	December 1963
		61342		BR Gorton Works	1000		January 1949	December 1966
		61343		BR Gorton Works	1001		February 1949	March 1966
		61344		BR Gorton Works	1002		March 1949	September 1966
		61345		BR Gorton Works	1003		April 1949	July 1966
		61346		BR Gorton Works	1004		April 1949	June 1964
		61347		BR Gorton Works	1005		May 1949	April 1967
		61348		BR Gorton Works	1006		June 1949	December 1965
		61349		BR Gorton Works	1007		July 1949	August 1966

Ordered November 1947

		61350		BR Darlington Works	2072		July 1949	November 1966
		61351		BR Darlington Works	2073		August 1949	July 1964
		61352		BR Darlington Works	2074		August 1949	October 1962
		61353		BR Darlington Works	2075		September 1949	August 1965
		61354		BR Darlington Works	2076		September 1949	April 1967
		61355		BR Darlington Works	2077		September 1949	June 1964
		61356		BR Darlington Works	2078		September 1949	July 1964
		61357		BR Darlington Works	2079		October 1949	June 1965
		61358		BR Darlington Works	2080		October 1949	December 1963
		61359		BR Darlington Works	2081		October 1949	December 1963

Ordered September 1948

		61360		North British	26819		March 1959	April 1966
		61361		North British	26820		Marh 1950	December 1965
		61362		North British	26821		March 1950	September 1962
		61363		North British	26822		April 1950	September 1962
		61364		North British	26823		April 1950	September 1962
		61365		North British	26824		April 1950	July 1965
		61366		North British	26825		April 1950	December 1962
		61367		North British	26826		April 1950	August 1965
		61368		North British	26827		April 1950	January 1962
		61369		North British	26828		May 1950	December 1963
		61370		North British	26829		October 1950	July 1965
		61371		North British	26830		October 1950	September 1962
		61372		North British	26841		December 1950	June 1965
		61373		North British	26842		December 1950	September 1962

Continued on next page

Continued from previous page

Original LNER No.	1946 LNER No.	BR No. Re No.	Date	Builder	Works/ Builder's No.	Name	Date Built	Date Withdrawn
		61374		North British	26833		February 1951	September 1963
		61375		North British	26834		February 1951	November 1963
		61376		North British	26835		April 1951	February 1962
		61377		North British	26836		May 1951	September 1962
		61378		North British	26837		May 1951	November 1963
		61379		North British	26838	Mayflower	June 1951	September 1962
		61380		North British	26839		August 1951	March 1962
		61381		North British	26840		September 1951	November 1962
		61382		North British	26831		September 1951	December 1964
		61383		North British	26832		October 1951	January 1963
		61384		North British	26843		October 1951	January 1966
		61385		North British	26844		October 1951	October 1965
		61386		North British	26845		October 1951	December 1966
		61387		North British	26846		November 1951	October 1965
		61388		North British	26847		November 1951	June 1967
		61389		North British	26848		November 1951	November 1965
		61390		North British	26849		December 1951	February 1966
		61391		North British	26850		December 1951	September 1962
		61392		North British	26851		December 1951	June 1965
		61393		North British	26852		January 1952	September 1963
		61394		North British	26853		January 1952	November 1965
		61395		North British	26854		February 1952	October 1962
		61396		North British	26855		February 1952	September 1965
		61397		North British	26856		March 1952	June 1965
		61398		North British	26857		March 1952	November 1964
		61399		North British	26858		April 1952	September 1963

Ordered February 1949

		61400		BR Darlington Works	2102		March 1950	December 1964
		61401		BR Darlington Works	2103		April 1950	April 1964
		61402		BR Darlington Works	2104		April 1950	June 1964
		61403		BR Darlington Works	2105		April 1950	July 1966
		61404		BR Darlington Works	2106		May 1950	November 1965
		61405		BR Darlington Works	2107		May 1950	September 1962
		61406		BR Darlington Works	2108		May 1950	April 1966
		61407		BR Darlington Works	2109		June 1950	April 1967
		61408		BR Darlington Works	2110		June 1950	December 1962
		61409		BR Darlington Works	2111		June 1950	September 1963

Notes

Locomotives built by the North British Locomotive Co. Ltd were constructed at their Queen's Park Works, Glasgow.

No. 61264 is now preserved on the Great Central Railway.

No. 61306 is now preserved on the Nene Valley Railway, and has been named *Mayflower*.

Upon withdrawal from service the following members of the class were transferred to Departmental Stock for use as Heating Boilers.

BR No.	Departmental No.	Date to Departmental Stock	Date Finally Withdrawn
61050	30	February 1966	April 1968
61051	31	February 1966	March 1966
61059	17	November 1963	April 1966
61105	27	March 1965	May 1966
61138	26	January 1965	October 1967
61181	18	November 1963	December 1965
61194	28	August 1965	June 1966
61204	19	November 1963	February 1966
61205	20	November 1963	January 1965
61233	21	November 1963	April 1966
61252	22	November 1963	May 1964
61264	29	November 1965	July 1967
61272	25	January 1965	November 1965
61300	23	November 1963	November 1965
61315	32	February 1966	April 1968
61375	24	November 1963	April 1966

Liveries

It was almost invariably railway company practice to paint new locomotives in Shop Grey for photographic purposes, at the time of initial construction, rebuilding or renumbering. This convention shows the second member of the class, No. 8302 *Eland*, when new at Darlington in June 1943. Built as works number 1912, it is in fully lined Works Grey, numbered and lettered in white. Ownership is shown simply as 'NE'. The lining of the wheels and cylinders is worthy of note. The locomotive was allocated to work the south east section and eventually had a working life of twenty years and three months.

National Railway Museum

Taken in September 1943, this photograph shows No. 8303 *Impala* in plain, unlined black with lettering and numbering in 12-inch white letters, unshaded. Ownership is shown again as 'NE', but this was extended to the full 'LNER' before Nationalisation. Officially, all the B1s were to be fitted with the Group Standard 4,200 gallon tender, but there were some variations. The records show that *Impala* was fitted with a new tender when built, but clearly the one shown here lacks the front coal rail of the Group Standard type.

National Railway Museum

Kudu was the last but one of the original Darlington built batch of B1s and is shown, above, in unlined works grey, with numbering and lettering in gold. In 1943 a complete renumbering scheme was planned for all London & North Eastern Railway locomotives, under which the B1s would be renumbered from 1000. The scheme was put into action in January 1946 when Nos 8302, 8303, 8304, 8307, 8308 and 8309 received their new identification. *Kudu* was chosen for photographic record and appears below in shop grey as 1008.

National Railway Museum

No. 1065 was photographed at Doncaster in 1947, in lined black livery. However, the tender is unlined with 'LNER' being in 12in letters, whereas the numbering on the cabside is in 10in letters. Built by the North British Locomotive Co. Ltd Nos 1040 to 1093 entered traffic with this anomaly.

P. Ransome-Wallis/National Railway Museum

At the beginning of November 1946 Darlington had just completed its batch of 30 new B1s, numbered 1010 to 1039: all were turned out in lined apple green with 12in modified Gill Sans yellow lettering. No. 1036 is seen here so arranged and named *Ralph Assheton* – the first named member of the class not to refer to an antelope.

National Railway Museum

No. 1098 was the only B1 delivered by the North British Locomotive Co. Ltd in August 1948 and is seen here leaving Potters Bar Tunnel with a 'down' local comprised of articulated sets. The numbering is clear upon the buffer-beam and legible on the cabside, but of ownership upon the tender there is no sign.
P. Ransome-Wallis/National Railway Museum

North British-built No. 1044 is seen in unlined black livery with 'LNER' in full on the tender at Norwich shed on 7th March 1948. This is an interesting point, as officially the locomotive entered traffic in April of that year.
A. R. Goult

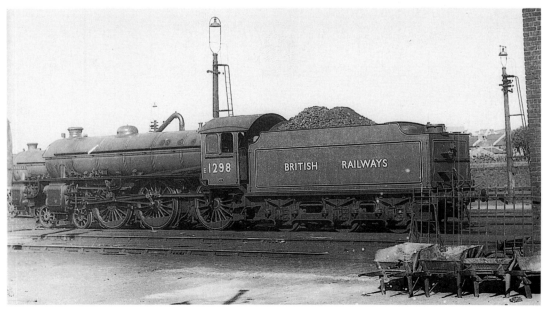

Five months into Nationalisation and the initial indecision over British Railways' numbering system is evident at Neasden shed. All engines taken into State ownership received a letter pre-fix to their number, identifying their region with the exception of ex-GWR examples: from February 1948 North British delivered new B1s to the Eastern Region pre-fixed 'E'. In fully lined apple green with 'BRITISH RAILWAYS' in full upon the tender, No. E1298 was photographed on 21st May, whilst an unidentifiable sister engine stands on the adjacent road.
A. R. Goult

During April 1948 Nos 61001 and 61009 participated at Stratford in trials of new emblems: by then, of course, it had been decided to advance all ex-LNER locomotives by 60,000, with one or two exceptions. *Eland* received the same emblem on both sides of the tender, consisting of a lion with its paw upon a wheel and seated upon a 'sausage' inscribed 'BRITISH RAILWAYS'. The lion faced forwards in both versions, which is heraldically incorrect for the right hand side.

National Railway Museum

Here we see the left hand side of B1, 61009 *Hartebeeste*, with the seated lion and wheel emblem between the words BRITISH RAILWAYS.

National Railway Museum

Finally, the right hand side of No. 61009 shows simply the seated lion-and-wheel facing forwards. None of these designs was used but a variation of that tested on No. 61001 became the familiar British Railways station totem sign.

National Railway Museum

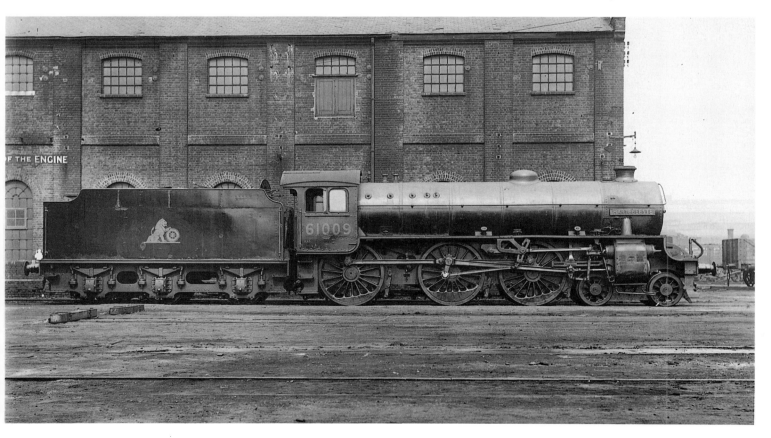

This one is very interesting: it is 5th March 1950, a little over two years into Nationalisation and No. 61200 is in work-stained, fully lined black livery, but there is no sign of ownership upon the tender. The train is the Sunday 2.06pm Cambridge to King's Cross stopping train, passing over Welwyn Viaduct. The following north-west wind makes an attractive exhaust pattern.

E. D. Bruton

The first 'official' British Railways livery applied to a B1 at Darlington. As they were designated mixed traffic locomotives the B1s were painted black, lined red, cream and grey, which livery is worn here by No. 61084. An emblem has still to be decided upon so 'BRITISH RAILWAYS' appears on the tender sides. The chosen livery for passenger stock was plum and spilt milk, and two rakes of coaches were painted in this colour scheme and used to test public reaction; one set was used on the "North Briton" and the train was often left in Newcastle station for this purpose.

National Railway Museum

No. 61400 is seen at Darlington in the first full mixed traffic livery of British Railways – black, lined red, cream and grey with the lion astride a driving wheel, standing upon a panel reading 'BRITISH RAILWAYS' – the famous 'anorexic lion'. Note the difference in the lining of the cab between this and on No. 61084 in the previous illustration.

National Railway Museum

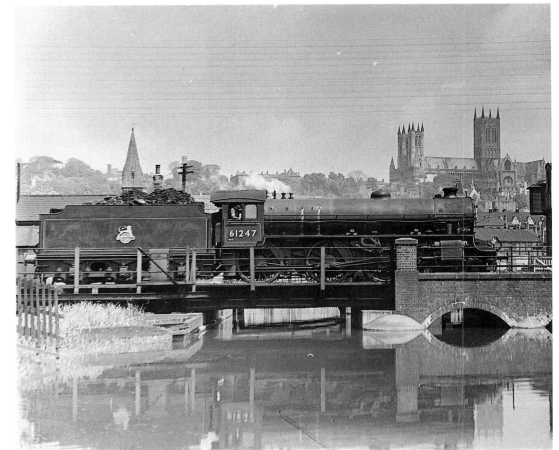

Against the back-drop of Lincoln Cathedral No. 61247 runs light engine across the River Witham. Included to show that the lion and wheel emblem faced forward on both sides of the tender. Built by the North British Locomotive Co. Ltd – builder's No. 26148 and named *Lord Burghley*, which begs the question – where were the nameplates?

P. Ransome-Wallis/National Railway Museum

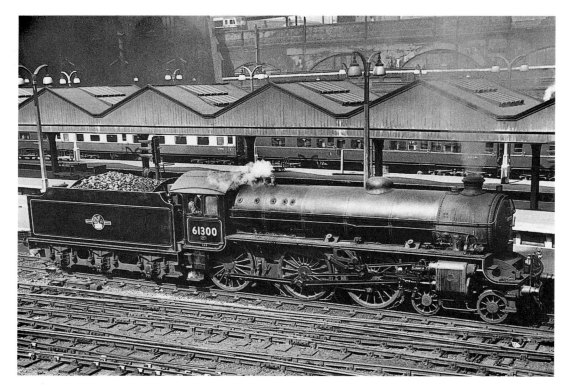

The final livery carried by the B1s. Black, lined red, cream and grey with the second British Railways emblem on the tender: the famous lion rising from a crown holding a driving wheel in its front paws, all within a circle and 'BRITISH RAILWAYS' on either side. At last the lion faced left all the time. No. 61300 is so adorned at Liverpool Street in 1959. Built by North British as No. E1300, builder's No. 26201, in March 1948, this was the last B1 but one to receive light repairs at Stratford, on 22nd June, 1960. It was withdrawn in November 1963. The last B1 to receive light repairs at the old Great Eastern works was No. 61109.

A. R. J. Frost

Bongo

It was intended that only those members of the class built in the Company's workshops should be named, together with the first of an order for locomotives from the North British Locomotive Co. Ltd, and all should be named after antelopes. Strangely, the old Stockton & Darlington name *Antebore* was not used. As has been said in the Introduction, almost from the day that No. 8306 entered traffic the class were known colloquially as "Bongos". The author feels quite sure that like him, precious few railway enthusiasts have any idea what a Bongo looks like – so here it is! The animal stands up to 4ft at the shoulder in the male, the coat being a beautiful chestnut red with prominent white stripes. Both sexes carry horns, which may be up to 13 and 9½ inches long in the male and female respectively. There are stout, smooth and spirally twisted. The Bongo is confined to equatorial forests of the Congo Basin, West Africa and the forests of Maa and Kenya. Whilst it is difficult to maintain accurate census, the Bongo does not appear on any of the IUCN threatened species categories.

Zoological Society of London

As No. 1005, *Bongo* passes New Southgate in 1946 with a King's Cross to Cambridge slow. Wartime conditions are evident for the locomotive is not at its cleanest and the tender still bears the simple inscription 'NE', which was a deliberate cost-cutting measure during hostilities.

Real Photographs

The Life of a Loco

No. 8301 emerged from Darlington Works against a number- less order (placed in August 1942), in December 1942 and without a works number. Close inspection of the works plate reveals the locomotive's running number and date of construction only. Although the locomotive was completed at Darlington, where it was photographed it was sent to Doncaster Works for official inspection on 13th December, and entered traffic on 19th December. This locomotive was named *Springbok*, ostensibly because of a recent visit to the United Kingdom by General Smuts, the then Prime Minister of South Africa. The locomotive was allocated to Gorton and ran in unlined black livery.

National Railway Museum

In February 1946 the engine became No. 1000, and in September 1947 was sent to Doncaster specifically for repainting in apple green, as seen here, in company with V2 2-6-2.

National Railway Museum

Springbok received the British Railways' number relatively early, becoming No. 61000 in May 1948. In the new guise the engine was photographed wearing the Colchester shed code 30E, but the location is unrecorded.

Real Photographs

Still allocated to Colchester, but wearing the final British Railways livery. No. 61000 was photographed at its home shed on 3rd November 1957. *Springbok* was withdrawn in March 1962 – under 20 years old – what a waste!

A. R. Goult

The First to Go

On 7th March 1950 No. 61057 was involved in an accident at Rivenhall End, when it ran into the rear of a freight train. The remains were removed to Stratford where they were photographed on the 18th of the month. On the adjacent road stands one of Hill's Great Eastern design, LNER modified and built, N7 0-6-2Ts, No. 69711. The insurance phraseology 'beyond economic repair' very clearly applies; the locomotive was condemned and withdrawn. Not surprisingly, it has the lowest recorded mileage of any B1: up to its last shopping in July 1949 the recorded mileage was 160,170, so it is unlikely to have exceeded 200,000 miles by the time of the accident. Many of the earlier North British B1s ran more than 100,000 miles before their first heavy repair, but No. 61057 covered only 18,931 miles from the time it was new in July 1946, to entering Stratford on 26th October for a heavy repair.

A. R. Goult

The right hand motion of No. 61059. This was the normal standard of cleanliness when Richard Hardy was shed master at Ipswich.   *H. N. James*

The left hand motion of No. 61026 *Ourebi* at Doncaster in December 1950. Clean – but not quite as spotless as No. 61059.

A. Garraway

From July to December 1950 Vulcan Foundry built No. 61164 was fitted with a chime whistle on the right hand side of the smoke box, for tests to determine a suitable whistle for the new Standard Pacifics. It is curious that a Neasden based locomotive should be taken to Doncaster for the trials. This picture was taken at Doncaster, shortly after the chime whistle was fitted, for it is dated July 1950.

A. Garraway

The cab of the pioneer B1, *Springbok*. As the number 1000 is inscribed upon the rear of the cab roof, the photograph dates from post February 1946. As can be seen, the cab has a level floor instead of the previously favoured well arrangement. A Great Central style regulator replaces Gresley's long established pull-out type with a handle at each side of the cab. Crew comfort has been thought of with the provision of bucket seats.

National Railway Museum

It was the intention of the London & North Eastern Railway to fit the post-war engines with electric lighting sets, as had been fitted to three A2/1 Pacifics and A1/1 No. 4470 *Great Northern*. Under this scheme, electrical power was obtained from a 6-volt alternator mounted on an extension to the rear bogie axle, with a battery provided in the cab for use when stationary. A panel in the cab allowed the driver to control the headlamps, and illumination was also provided for the gauges and reversing gear indicator. Metropolitan-Vickers Electrical Co. was to supply the equipment but pressure of export orders prevented them from doing so. Couple to this the fact that in use, some of the alternators already fitted fell off the axle onto the permanent way, and so it was not surprising that the decision was taken to fit steam-operated generators instead. No. 1046 was so fitted in October 1946, with the Stones generator taken from Class C1 Atlantic No. 4448. It is seen here fitted on the right hand running plate, beside the smokebox. The engine is running Royal Train headcode: note the exceptional length of the lamp irons.

National Railway Museum

Titled Trains

The "East Anglian". In Coronation Year, 1937, the LNER decided to extend the era of streamlined trains to East Anglia. However, when the schedules appeared they proved to be something of an anticlimax for the 'down' train was scheduled to leave Liverpool Street at 6.40pm, calling at Ipswich from 8pm to 8.04pm, and reach Norwich Thorpe at 8.55pm. Similarly the 'up' train was pedestrianly scheduled. The vicissitudes of War dictated the withdrawal of the service, which was reinstated on 6th October 1946, with the same departure time from Liverpool Street. No. 1048 is seen awaiting departure, a little over six months after the reinstatement of the services, on 26th April 1947, bearing the LNER-style headboard.

LCGB/Ken Nunn Collection

On 12th June 1951 British Railways used a Dynamometer car on the "East Anglian" in preparation for the speeding up of the titled trains on the Great Eastern section, which the introduction of the 'Britannia' Pacifics would allow. Above, North British built No. 61270 is seen leaving Ipswich Tunnel with the 'up' train. As luck would have it the 'down' train, below, was photographed later in the day as it left Liverpool Street still at 6.40pm. The British Railways' headboard is markedly different to the LNER one.

H. N. James and LCGB/Ken Nunn Collection

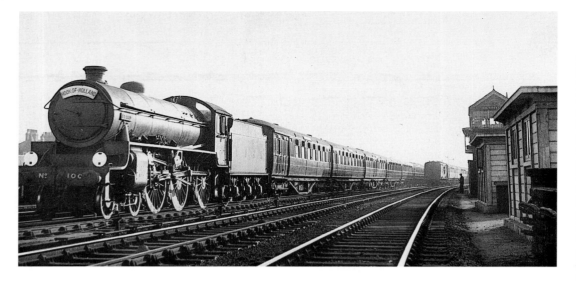

Prior to its absorption into the LNER, it is generally agreed that the height of the Great Eastern Railway's achievements were the Continental boat services. Of these the peak was the Hook of Holland service, which was the principal means of communication between England and the whole of North Germany and beyond. The service was steadily improved by the LNER: the Second World War seeing the suspension of the service but this was reinstated in the timetable three times weekly in November 1945, and daily a year later. Bearing the headboard, "Hook of Holland", the second B1, No. 1001 *Eland*, takes the 8pm 'down' departure to Parkeston Quay, past Bethnal Green, on the evening of 28th April 1947. In later LNER days the train became officially, the "Hook Continental", and the 'down' train's departure time from Liverpool Street was moved to 8.30pm. The 'up' train left Parkeston Quay at 6.45am and was due into Liverpool Street at 7.53am. On 22nd July 1950, Vulcan Foundry built No. 61144 brought the overnight travellers from the Continent into the Capital. The headboard caries the Dutch and British flags.

LCGB/Ken Nunn Collection

The "Broadsman" ran from Cromer via Norwich Thorpe and Ipswich to Liverpool Street. The 'down' train departed the Capital at 3.40pm: on 24th March 1951 No. 61332, built by North British Locomotive Co. Ltd, waits to depart for Norfolk. In the summer time-tables that year the service was taken over by the 'Britannia' Pacifics.

LCGB/Ken Nunn Collection

In the summer of 1950 the only train not to stop at Ipswich in British Railways' days, was inaugurated to run from Liverpool Street to Beccles in 135 minutes for the 109¼ miles. The new service received the title "The Easterling". The 'up' train was allowed 145 minutes. It was a summer only service, and on a Saturday in 1952, the 'down' train passes Bealings in the capable hands of No. 61233.

H. N. James

It is perhaps stretching a point to include the "Oyster Special" under 'Titled Trains', but it did run regularly to mark the opening of the Oyster season. On 27th October 1950 No. 61109, from the first batch of B1s built by North British, is turned at Colchester shed.

LCGB/Ken Nunn Collection

With the introduction of the Summer 1949 timetables the title "The Fenman" was inaugurated. The new service departed Hunstanton at 6.45am calling at all stations on the 15½ miles to King's Lynn which was reached at 7.21am. Here the train reversed, leaving for London at 7.30am, and stopping at Downham Market and Ely it strolled across the Fenland to materialize at Cambridge an hour and a minute later, where a portion from Bury St Edmunds was attached having arrived ten minutes after the main section of the train. With similar alacrity the train was assembled, leaving for Liverpool Street at 8.48am, the Capital eventually being achieved at 10.30am. The distance from Hunstanton of 112½ miles took the quite incredible time of 3 hours 18 minutes – the train nevertheless was blessed with an express headcode as can be seen with No. 61283 passing Barnwell Junction with the "Fenman" on 25th June 1958. A similarly leisurely trip occurred on the northbound train.

LCGB/Ken Nunn Collection

"The Scandinavian" was another of the London & North Eastern Railway's Continental services run for the benefit of passengers bound for Denmark. The service lasted into British Railways' days, and on 9th July 1955, departed from the imposing station at Parkeston Quay at 1.30pm behind No. 61233 making its second appearance in this book.

Philip J. Kelley

The "Flushing Continental" of LNER fame became "The Day Continental", leaving Liverpool Street at 10.05am in summer and 9.33am in winter, running non-stop to Parkeston Quay West. On 24th March 1952 No. 61363 passes Manningtree with the 'down' train. The boiler is one of those bearing a smokebox door with narrow spaced hinges necessitating the fitting of the numberplate higher than was usual.

H. N. James

The use of a B1 on a Pullman train was a rare happening, occurring usually only when the scheduled locomotive had failed. On 12th August 1953 No. 60030 *Golden Fleece* had failed at Hitchin (an A4 *failed?*) with the "Tees-Tyne Pullman". New England based B1 No. 61207, with a self-cleaning smokebox, was pressed into service to take the train on.

A. Garraway

On 16th September 1955 Dundee based No. 61293 was at Glasgow's Eastfield shed wearing the "Fife Coast Express" headboard. Since the Second World War the train had become a Glasgow to St Andrews express only. On the adjacent road stands Gresley's A3 No. 60099 *Call Boy*, wearing "The North Briton" headboard.

Philip J. Kelley

Between the wars there had been a very popular breakfast express on the Great Central section of the LNER which left Sheffield for Marylebone at 7.30am, stopping only at Nottingham and Leicester, and into the Capital by 10.40am. Following the cessation of hostilities a morning express on the same route reappeared, which in the winter timetable of 1947, received the title "The Master Cutler". Clothed in apple green No. 1223 passes North Harrow very early in the new train's life, on 13th October 1947, with the morning service for Marylebone. Note the LNER style headboard.

LCGB/Ken Nunn Collection

The 'down' "Master Cutler" departed Marylebone at 6.15pm. On 1st June 1950, Leicester based No. 61187 passes Wembley Hill wearing the British Railways' style headboard.

LCGB/Ken Nunn Collection

In May 1948 a new title appeared on a Marylebone – Bradford express, "The South Yorkshireman", departing at 4.50pm. Here North British built No. 61383 crests the 1 in 100 Bagthorpe Bank, north of Nottingham, with the 'down' train.

D. B. Swale

The Pride of Ipswich

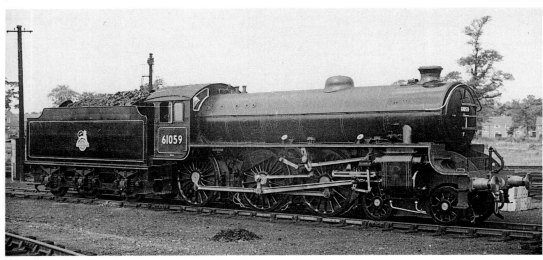

No. 61059 was built by North British Locomotive Co. Ltd and put into traffic in July 1946. Whilst at Ipswich shed under the auspices of R. H. N. (Dick) Hardy the locomotive was always kept in immaculate condition as this photograph shows.

H. N. James

Three remarkable men on No. 61059. From left to right: Claude Sansom, Shop Officeman; Jack Percy, Chargehand Fitter and Alderman A. G. Percy. Mr. Sansom was a Great Central man having been a fireman at Neasden and Gorton, and came to Ipswich for his driver's check in the 1920's, rising to the Manchester link at the time it was disbanded due to the war. Jack Percy had been an apprentice at Ipswich and came, in the words of Dick Hardy, to know everything there was to know about any engine. Finally, Arthur Percy who gave much of his life to public service, had a day job as the safety valve and gauge frame fitter which was flexible enough to allow him time off from duty. At one time he was the Mayor of Ipswich.

H. N. James

On 21st June 1951 the staff of Ipswich was 'on parade', assembled on and around the locomotive.   *H. N. James*

No. 61059 on Belstead Bank with an express for the Capital.   *H. N. James*

The regular crew of No. 61059, Driver Frank Cocksedge and Fireman George Lown. Mr Lown later became Train Crew Supervisor, eventually retiring in 1989.

H. N. James

No. 61059 was withdrawn from capital stock in November 1963 and transferred to departmental use, where it became No. 17. It is perhaps ironic that the once pride of the shed should return to Ipswich to see out its final days used for carriage heating. Final withdrawal came in April 1966.

H. N. James

On Shed

At King's Cross 'Top Shed' No. 61139, home based, stands alongside Gresley's Class V2 2-6-2 No. 60912, being prepared for a turn of duty. This would probably have been back to its home shed of New England (35A) at Peterborough. The date was 9th May 1954.

E. D. Bruton

The same engine – a very different location: No. 61139 was photographed nearly two years earlier on 15th June 1952 at Eastbourne Motive Power Depot, after working a Hitchin to Eastbourne excursion in the hands of Driver Edwards of Hornsey. This was the first working of a B1 to the South Coast. Built in April 1947 No. 61139 was the last of the first batch of B1s built by the North British Locomotive Co. Ltd. Behind the B1 stands No. 31866, one of Maunsell's N class 2-6-0s built for the South Eastern & Chatham Railway from 1917.

S. C. Nash

In immaculate ex-works condition No. 61054 stands at Stratford shed on 5th June 1958.

R. C. Riley

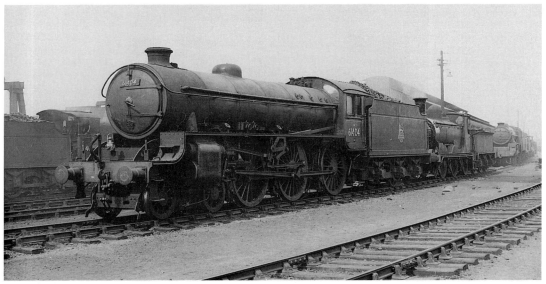

Darlington built No. 61404 stands at Glasgow's Corkerhill shed (67A) on 10th July 1955, surrounded by ex-London Midland & Scottish Railway shed-mates.

T. J. Edgington

Stratford again – prototype B1 No. 61000 *Springbok* was photographed on 6th September 1950, in company with No. 64680, one of Hill's J20 0-6-0s of the Great Eastern Railway.

A. R. Goult

Built in Glasgow in April 1948 by North British No. 61313 strayed about as far south as it was possible to go with a pigeon special on 26th June 1964. The location is again, Eastbourne Motive Power Depot, the 41B shed code, Sheffield Darnall, indicating that the special originated in Yorkshire. The shed-mate is equally far from home.

S. C. Nash

No. 61140 was the first of the class to be built by the Vulcan Foundry, entering service as LNER No. 1140 in April 1947, becoming No. 61140 in January 1949. In this picture the locomotive is seen at Glasgow Eastfield on 11th July 1954 attached to coal-weighing tender No. 4219. No. 61140 had this tender from April to July 1952 and then from September 1952 until the locomotive was withdrawn in December 1966.

A. R. Goult

By 29th June 1947 the days of the London & North Eastern Railway were numbered when No. 1108 was photographed at Neasden beside the turntable. The engine was barely six months old, having entered traffic in December 1946. The picture serves to remind what a dirty place a steam locomotive shed was, with piles of ashes lying around.

A. R. Goult

No. 61005 *Bongo* 'at home' at Cambridge shed, fairly late in life for the tender has the second British Railways' emblem and there are overhead wire warnings on the running plate. On the adjacent road stands one of R. A. Riddles' ex-WD 2-8-0s, No. 90138, with another behind the B1.

Real Photographs

No. 61354 from St Margarets (Edinburgh) has strayed to the Southern Region on 21st June 1953, where it was photographed at Stewarts Lane depot.

H. N. James

Immaculate in LNER apple green, No. 1207 was caught at Carstairs (which became 64D under British Railways), on 30th June 1947.

T. J. Edgington

On 30th April 1956 No. 61399 (the very last B1 built by North British) was being cleaned for Royal Train duty at Stratford.

Philip J. Kelley

At Immingham shed No. 61406 stands cold on 7th August 1965. Built at Darlington in May 1950 the engine had eight months of life left when photographed.

T. J. Edgington

'At home' at Thornton Junction, LNER built No. 61029 *Chamois* stands near the coaling tower in August 1966. Whilst the shed code worn by the engine is 62A the inscription on the bufferbeam reads 'St Margarets' – perhaps the chalk arrow serves to remind someone that an amendment is required. A B1 on former North British Railway's territory.

D. B. Swale

Left: The scene is again Thornton Junction, with an unidentified J38 sandwiched between a pair of "Bongos", both of which were LNER built, No. 61347, nearest the camera had come from Gorton as works No. 1005 in May 1949, and No. 61354 (works No. 2076) from Darlington in September 1949. Both were destined to be withdrawn in April 1967.

D. B. Swale

Named Locomotives

Above: The 14th member of the class, No. 61013 *Topi* – very nearly the shortest name on a British locomotive, at Darlington shed ex-works.

H. N. James

As the independent existence of the LNER drew to its close the company embarked upon a policy of naming locomotives after some of the company's directors, as had happened before the Grouping. Thus, No. 1249 was named *Fitzherbert Wright* when the locomotive entered traffic in October 1947 following delivery from the North British Locomotive Co. Ltd and finished in the LNER's passenger locomotive livery of lined apple green. The gentleman admiring the engine is none other than Arthur Peppercorn, the last Chief Mechanical Engineer of the LNER. He held the position from 1946 to 1947 (succeeding Edward Thompson) and was appointed similarly for British Railways Eastern and North Eastern Regions from 1948 to 1949, when the post was abolished.

National Railway Museum

No. 1189 was the last B1 built by Vulcan Foundry and the only one from that builder to receive a name – again after one of the LNER's directors – *Sir William Gray*. The cabside number appears curiously closely spaced. The engine had a working life of under 20 years, being withdrawn in May 1967.

National Railway Museum

No. 61251 *Oliver Bury* was the last North British built member of the class to receive a name at the time it entered traffic. Its main claim to fame is its participation in the 1948 Locomotive Exchanges, when it was the most economical mixed traffic engine in the London, Midland Region tests. It is seen here in company with a WD 2-8-0.

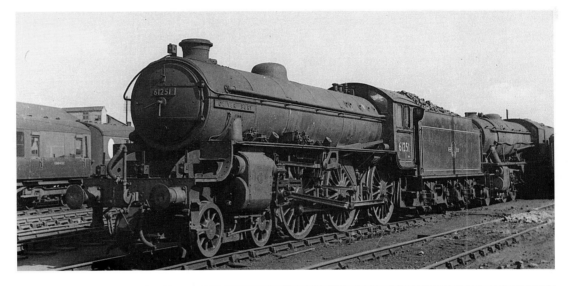

Whilst the subject of the previous illustration was the last North British built locomotive to receive a name at the time of entering traffic, No. 61379 was the very last member of the class to be named. 'At home' at Immingham, 40B *Mayflower* bears a plaque on the cabside which reads 'This locomotive was named "Mayflower" 13th July 1951 as a symbol of the ties between the two towns of Boston and the lasting friendship between the U.S.A. and the British Commonwealth'. A nameplate and a plaque were mounted and presented to the Mayor and Council of Boston on 5th December 1962, the engine having been withdrawn in September of that year. The drive to the speedometer can be seen on the rear crankpin.

Real Photographs

North British built No. 61244 *Strang Steel* of St Margaret's shed, at Dalmeny Junction with Class 'C' headcode, but hauling a train consisting of passenger stock. The boiler is equipped with a self-cleaning smokebox.

P. Ransome-Wallis/National Railway Museum

Gnu is unquestionably the shortest name carried by a British Railways locomotive, on No. 61018, although equally short names had been employed by the GWR (*Wye*), LNWR (*Bee*) and LMSR (*H.L.I.*). The scene is York shed.

D. B. Swale

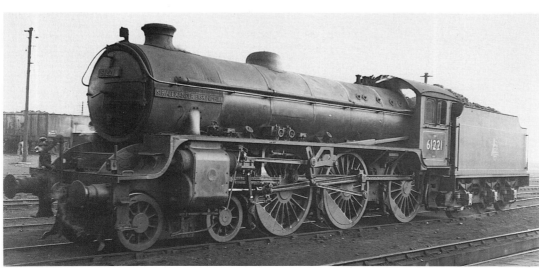

No. 61221 had the longest name of any B1, *Sir Alexander Erskine-Hill*. In order to accommodate the names within the length of the smokebox, considerably smaller than usual letters were used.

Real Photographs

In immaculate condition to work a Railway Correspondence & Travel Society special, No. 61031 *Reedbuck* was photographed at Battersby Junction on 2nd May 1964.

T. J. Edgington

The Great Eastern

No. 61004 *Gazelle* backs down the throat to Liverpool Street to take the 'down' "Day Continental" to Parkeston Quay. As departure time was 9.23am this would probably have been a little after 9am.

R. C. Riley

Above: On 24th March 1951 No. 61363, lacking any decent polish, lifted the "Day Continental" past Forest Gate on its way to the Essex coast. Speed at this point was about 40 mph in conditions of slight haze and no sun, which would have lightened the high blue-brick retaining wall, to say the least!

E. D. Bruton

Right: On 24th July 1962 No. 61149 was captured rounding the curve at Manningtree to join the main line with an 'up' relief Continental Express from Parkeston Quay to Liverpool Street.

H. N. James

Below: The "East Anglian", having been re-instated to the timetable on 7th October 1946 is seen with the LNER style headboard, in the hands of black-liveried No. 1048.

East Anglian Daily Times

No. 61048 climbs away from Ipswich with the 1.20pm to Great Yarmouth on 1st September 1951.   *B. Reading*

Under lowering skies with a marvellous exhaust, No. 61378 passes Bentley with a Harwich to Peterborough express in March 1959.   *A. R. J. Frost*

Ignominy indeed! No. 61332 has failed with a hot box at Chelmsford and is about to be replaced by one of Holden's J15 class 0-6-0s No. 65448. The train is the 11.40am Norwich to Liverpool Street express and the date is 2nd October 1948. Neither locomotive has yet received a smokebox numberplate, the numbers still being painted upon the bufferbeams.

LCGB/Ken Nunn Collection

In the last days of the London & North Eastern Railway No. 1049 skirts the River Orwell approaches to Ipswich with the 'down' "East Anglian". The stock is probably the set built especially for the train before the outbreak of the Second World War.

East Anglian Daily Times

No. 61119 again passes Bentley Junction with the 10.33am London to Great Yarmouth express on 21st June 1959.

A. R. J. Frost

The "Easterling" heads for Beccles and Great Yarmouth past Kelvedon, in the charge of No. 61234 on 29th July 1950. This was the 10.36am ex-Liverpool Street.

LCGB/Ken Nunn Collection

No. 61048 passes Baylham Suffolk with an express for Liverpool Street in the summer of 1952.   *H. N. James*

No. 61149 passes Baylham with a freight from Parkeston Quay to Whitemoor on 21st April 1958.

H. N. James

On 26th April 1958 immaculate Norwich (32A) based No. 61045 passes Trumpington with an 'up' excursion, bearing reporting number 552.

R. C. Riley

At Channelsea Junction on 22nd July 1951 North British built No. 61252 is about to change engines with Stanier "Black 5" No. 45092, which had arrived with the 9.30am Watford to Clacton special.

LCGB/Ken Nunn Collection

Having exited Ipswich Tunnel No. 61254 approaches Halifax Junction with an express for London.

H. N. James

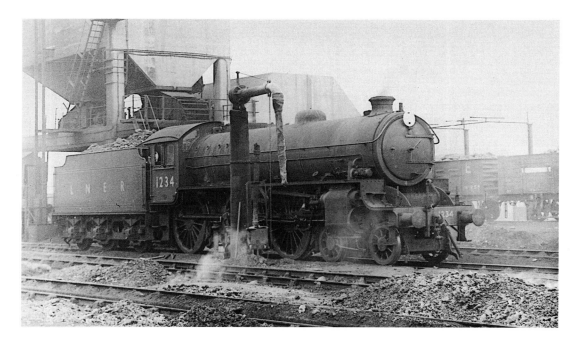

A simple one for spotters to remember, North British built No. 1234 stands beside a water crane amidst the grime of Norwich shed on 7th March 1948: Nationalisation may have come but the engine still proudly wears LNER apple green livery.

A. R. Goult

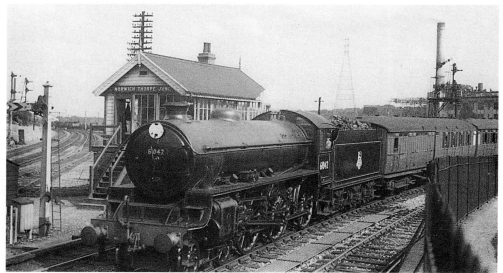

The third member of the class built by North British, No. 61042, passes Norwich Thorpe Junction box on 25th August 1950, with a 'down' stopping passenger train.

H. N. James

During March and April 1951 Nos 61370 and 61373 worked a series of dynamometer car tests over the level section between New England and Grimsby. Similar tests were carried out until mid June between Whitemoor and Norwich. The train worked double-headed, the leading engine carrying an anemometer at the front to measure the relative wind velocity, and also a wind-direction indicator.

Twixt New England and Peterborough coaching stock was used but between Whitemoor and Norwich freight stock was employed. Around 20 round trips were made. The test train is seen at Wensum Junction on 31st May 1951.

LCGB/Ken Nunn Collection

No. 61203, from the second North British built batch of engines, passes Ponders End with the 'down' "Fenman" on 10th May 1960. Based at 31A Cambridge, this locomotive has a self-cleaning smokebox, but the express lacks a headboard.

Collection R. C. Riley

In the summer of 1951 No. 61119 passes Mountnessing in Essex with the 'down' "Day Continental".

Real Photographs

Some way from its home shed of New England, No. 61113 waits at Cromer Beach with the Ian Allan Trains Illustrated "Fenlands Express" on 19th September 1954.

E. D. Bruton

No. 61044 reaches Wroxham with the 'down' "Broadsman" on 12th May 1953. Based at Norwich shed, the locomotive sports what would normally be Class 'J' headcode – mineral or empty wagon train, but here it is the Cromer route code.

Philip J. Kelley

'Neath the wires No. 61378 crests Brentwood Summit with a 'down' express for Norwich on 14th June 1958.

A. R. Goult

With a badly scorched smokebox door and a very black exhaust, No. 61058 passes Bentley Junction with an 'up' express from Norwich in 1959.

A. R. J. Frost

Parkeston Quay West on 9th July 1955: No. 61233 arrives with the 9.30am ex-Liverpool Street, the "Day Continental", whilst No. 61109 is in charge of the relief train.

LCGB Ken Nunn Collection/Philip J. Kelley

No. 61055 is seen near Bentley with a Norwich Thorpe to Liverpool Street milk train in 1950.

A. R. J. Frost

No. 61300 makes an appearance climbing Brentwood Bank with an express to Norwich on 14th June 1948.

A. R. Goult

Stratford based No. 61235 passes Westerfield Junction with a Holiday Camp Express for Gorleston-on-Sea in 1952.

H. N. James

No. 61378 emerges from the ornate portal of Audley End Tunnel with the 10.41am Caister to Liverpool Street express on 9th July 1958.

LCGB/Ken Nunn Collection

No. 61252 runs light engine past Bentley Junction in January 1959.   *A. R. J. Frost*

No. 61058 at Yarmouth South Town with the 6.19pm express for Liverpool Street on 1st October 1955.
                                                                                      Philip J. Kelley

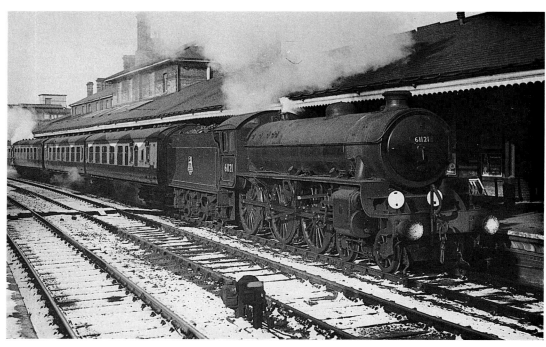

On a snowy 30th January 1954 No. 61121 moves away from Ipswich with the empty London, Midland Region stock of a Birmingham to Ipswich football excursion.

H. N. James

Approaching Bentley station on 4th January 1959 No. 61270 has the 8.20am Sundays only Peterborough North to Colchester express.

A. R. J. Frost

The Great Central

With a three-coach non-corridor rake of ex-LNER stock labelled 'Basford' on the end, slightly leaking but well polished No. 61390 (of the final batch built by North British) from Colwick (38A) Motive Power Depot, eases away from the stop at Nottingham Arkwright Street with the 3.50pm Nottingham Victoria to Leicester Central 'all Stations' Class 'B' passenger job. The date is 15th May 1954.

E. D. Bruton

The afternoon of 15th May 1954 was cloudy as North British built No. 61096 passes through Arkwright Street station, Nottingham with an 'up' train under Class 'A' express passenger headcode.

E. D. Bruton

Sheffield Victoria on 21st September 1958 Vulcan Foundry built B1 No. 61165 of 41F Mexborough and now preserved ex-Great Central Railway D11 class 4-4-0 No. 62660 *Butler-Henderson* have charge of a Railway Correspondence & Travel Society special. On the adjacent road stands a Gresley K3/3 2-6-0 No. 61802.

T. J. Edgington

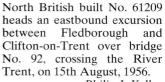

North British built No. 61209 heads an eastbound excursion between Fledborough and Clifton-on-Trent over bridge No. 92, crossing the River Trent, on 15th August, 1956.

Philip J. Kelley

No. 61188 passes through Bagthorpe Junction with a Colwick bound coal train in 1964.

D. B. Swale

No. 61311 heads an eastbound express over the River Trent, between Cottam and Torksey on 22nd August 1956.
Philip J. Kelley

The sixth B1 built by the North British Locomotive Co. Ltd, No. 61045, near Tuxford approaches High Marnham with an eastbound coal train in July 1962.
D. B. Swale

Vulcan Foundry built No. 61151. Here it is seen south of Bulwell Common with a Sheffield to Marylebone express.
D. B. Swale

Showing a very work-stained smokebox door No. 61151 of 41A Sheffield Darnall pilots V2 2-6-2 south of Bulwell Common with an 'up' Sheffield to Marylebone express.

D. B. Swale

At the north end of Nottingham Victoria No. 61173 manoeuvres to take water before working the "Great Central Rail Tour" on 3rd September 1964.

D. B. Swale

In August 1964 No. 61167 was photographed at Trent Lane Junction with a Nottingham Victoria to Crewe parcels train.

D. B. Swale

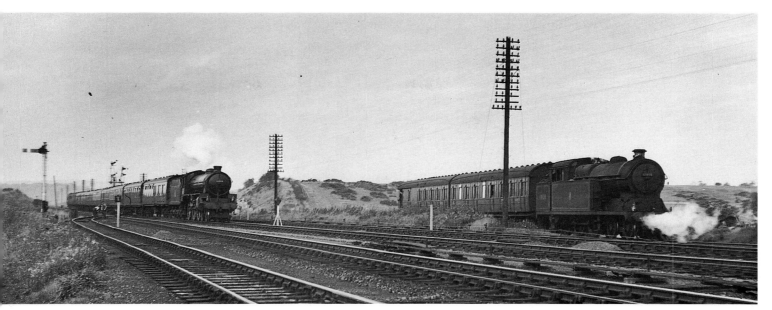

On 9th October 1958 Class A5 4-6-2T No. 69818 waits at signals north of Bulwell Common with "Dido" workmens' train from Annesley Motive Power Depot, as B1 No. 61033 *Dibatag* heads south with an 'up' York to Bournemouth express.

D. B. Swale

No. 61248 *Geoffrey Gibbs* with an 'up' coal train departs from Bulwell South Junction in 1965.

D. B. Swale

LNER built No. 61003 *Gazelle* moves a train of coal out of the 'down' sidings at Bulwell South Junction for Colwick in July 1965.

D. B. Swale

Great Central/ Lancashire & Yorkshire Joint

On 5th September 1954 Vulcan Foundry built No. 61156 approaches Penistone with the 9.20am Heath and Chesterfield to Blackpool Central excursion No. 310.

Philip J. Kelley

Doncaster (36A) based No. 61114 leaves Penistone with the 9.40am, ex-Manchester London Road to Sheffield express on 5th September 1954. Two B1s can be seen in the distance, with No. 61327 on the right.

Philip J. Kelley

The Midland

On 10th May 1950 No. 61318 is seen entering Castle Bromwich station with the 6.52am Cleethorpes to Birmingham New Street. The train is about to make the special stop for British Industries Fair passengers. The nicely polished locomotive is Immingham (40B) based and carries the then still new lion and wheel emblem.

E. D. Bruton

Also Immingham based, No. 61042 was the third member of the class built by the North British Locomotive Co. Ltd. It is seen here at Nottingham shed requiring attention, having been taken off a Birmingham New Street to Cleethorpes working.

D. B. Swale

No. 61195 came from the second batch of B1s built by North British. On 20th October 1953 it had brought the 6.53am from Cleethorpes into Birmingham New Street.

T. J. Edgington

No. 61305 is held at signals on 5th September 1954 in Beeston Yard whilst working a Normanton goods.

D. B. Swale

No. 61302 at Netherfield and Colwick with an RCTS special on 26th March 1966, wearing Class 'G' headlamp code, but no shed code.

T. J. Edgington

Within the gloom of Birmingham New Street on 26th April 1955 No. 61190, the first of North British Locomotive Co. Ltd's second batch, has arrived with the 6.57am from Cleethorpes.

T. J. Edgington

The Great Northern

In early winter sunshine a rather stained No. 61203, still lettered 'British Railways' lopes up the fast line near Potters Bar station with the 8.50am semi-fast ex-Peterborough, at about 35 mph. The train consists of sundry articulated pieces and sets of Gresley suburbans. The date is 4th December 1949.

E. D. Bruton

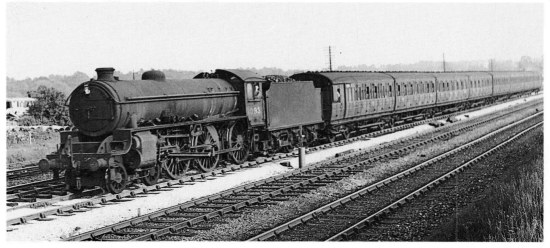

In the 'Golden Summer' of 1947 (although only in May) at 7pm British Double Summer Time, on 23rd of that month, No. 1093, showing the usual postwar grime, heads a local train, probably for Hitchin of Peterborough, north of Hatfield near to the North Orbital Road to Hertford overbridge.

E. D. Bruton

No. 1198 in post war grubby condition heads for King's Cross, just south of Brookmans Park station on 5th October 1947 with an 'up' Class 'B' stopping train from Peterborough.

E. D. Bruton

In 1949 No. 1230 was caught at Doncaster, still in London & North Eastern Railway livery.

A. Garraway

No. 61003 *Gazelle* waits outside Derby Friargate with a train of empty hoppers for Colwick in September 1964.

D. B. Swale

On 25th July 1959 the third member of the class to be built by Vulcan Foundry, No. 61142, was photographed near Hatfield with an 'up' Grimsby and Cleethorpes express.

Philip. J. Kelley

The 'down' 2.25pm King's Cross to Cambridge "Buffet Car Express" approaches Potters Bar Tunnel on 22nd April 1950, headed by No. 61266. The King's Cross based locomotive is one of the series fitted with electric head lamps whilst, with the exception of the buffet car, the train is composed entirely of standard Gresley stock.

E. D. Bruto

The final batch of ten B1s was built at Darlington between March and June 1950. The very last was No. 61409 which is seen here at Belle Isle, King's Cross with an 'up' express.

R. C. Riley

On 11th November 1951 No. 61266 rounds the reverse curves just south of Hatfield with a Class 'C' express fully-fitted perishables train. The engine is showing use of the self-cleaning smokebox judging by the muck plastered around the outside! Although the wind is slightly the wrong way, the light smoke haze remains nicely air-borne.

E. D. Bruton

No. 61190, the last of the second batch of B1s built by North British, bursts under the Hertford road bridge on the northern outskirts of Hatfield, at 60mph with a 'down' special (reporting No. 317), on 29th June 1951. The train is on the Down Main line, the nearer track is the Down Slow and that on the right is the single line Hatfield/Welwyn Garden City/Luton and Dunstable branch which made an end-on connection with the ex-London & North Western Railway branch from Leighton Buzzard. On the far side, beyond the 'up' lines, is the single line branch to Cole Green and Hertford, again via Welwyn Garden City. The smokebox shows either signs of priming or use of the self-cleaning facility.

E. D. Bruton

Between Leen Valley Junction and Basford North, viewed from the Great Central line, No. 61163 proceeds with a Colwick to Burton goods on 18th October 1958.

D. B. Swale

No. 61097 (from 34D, Hitchin Motive Power Depot) hustles the 1.55pm Hitchin to King's Cross Class 'B' passenger train from the depths of Potters Bar Tunnel on 20th March 1957. The engine is accelerating down the 1 in 200 after the station stop and has reached about 45 mph on leaving the tunnel.

E. D. Bruton

No. 61392 and Gresley B17/4 No. 61657 *Doncaster Rovers* double head a King's Cross to Cambridge express through Harringay in 1958. A batch of the North British built B1s had the smokebox door hinges close together, necessitating the fitment of the top lamp bracket somewhat higher than usual. Presumably this is the reason for the fitting of the footstep below and to the left of the shed plate on this New England based B1. The B17 was built by the LNER.
P. Ransome-Wallis/National Railway Museum

King's Cross (34A) allocated No. 61137 heads for home with the 'up' Sunday 8.50am semi-fast from Peterborough at 11am on 5th March 1950. Two coaches in 'blood and custard' have appeared in the rake of eight vehicles. The scene is the North Orbital-Hertford Road (A414) overbridge north of Hatfield.
E. D. Bruton

Immingham 40B based No. 61168 passes New Southgate with an express on 3rd May 1958. In contrast to the preceding picture a single coach lingers in carmine and cream.
A. R. Goult

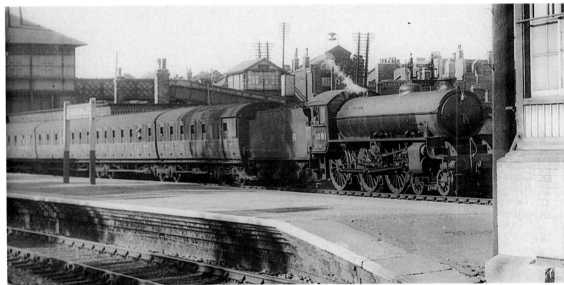

Nationalisation is but four and a half months old so No. 1091 retains its LNER livery at Harringay, on 18th May 1948 with a Gresley articulated set.
A. R. Goult

The eleven-coach 4pm King's Cross to Grimsby and Cleethorpes express (just having cleared Hadley Wood North Tunnel) heads for Potters Bar Tunnel at about 40 mph up the 1 in 200 in the charge of Immingham (40B) based No. 61284. Eight of the coaches are in carmine and cream, whilst the tender wears the then new lion and wheel emblem. Shot in soft sunshine on 22nd April 1950.
E. D. Bruton

On 7th January 1951 No. 61325 storms through Brookmans Park with the 'up' Sunday 11.05am Cambridge / King's Cross express at around 50 mph. The locomotive is fitted with a steam operated generator and electric lighting, although daymaker oil lamps are also carried to assist signalmen on train recognition. Note that the smokebox door lamp position has no electric lamp but that it is fitted 'atop' the smokebox in front of the chimney.

E. D. Bruton

Hitchin Motive Power Depot (34D) based No. 61095 swings up to Red Hill signals on the Down Fast line with the 6.10pm King's Cross to Peterborough stopping train, logged at 60 mph on the evening of 2nd May 1951 at 6.55pm. An 'up' train is signalled on the left of the scene.

E. D. Bruton

Making 'even time' No. 61373 passes the Hertford Road overbridge north of Hatfield, heading towards Lea Viaduct with a Class 'A' 'down' relief, or special reporting No. 321, at 8.07pm on Friday 29th July 1951. Note the vintage distant signal, right.

E. D. Bruton

On the first day of Spring – 21st March 1953 No. 61151 heads an 'up' Saturday special (reporting No. 850) under Marshmoor Bridge and out of its own exhaust at about 40 mph as it is about to overtake an 'up' freight. A 'down' line train is signalled on the Fast.

E. D. Bruton

Passing the attractive cluster of Great Northern Railway somersault signals and with Greenwood signal box in the middle distance, Hitchin (34D) based No. 61090 is working home with the 'down' 2.21pm outer suburban stopping train from King's Cross. The locomotive is somewhat grubby. A train is due on the 'up' line and has been routed by the signalmen to the Up Slow line at the resumption of four tracks by the signal box on 7th July 1951.

E. D. Bruton

On 21st April 1951 No. 61113 leaves Hadley Wood North Tunnel with the 'down' 9.05am King's Cross to Cambridge "Buffet Car Express". No ownership details are visible on the tender.

E. D. Bruton

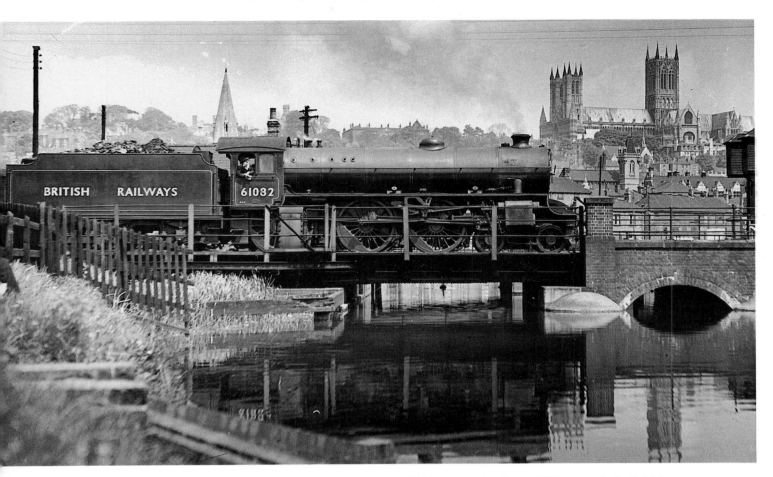

Against the glorious back-drop of Lincoln Cathedral No. 61082 crosses the River Witham early in British Railways ownership.

P. Ransome Wallis/National Railway Museum

No. 61082 passes Gosberton with a March to Lincoln Class 'B' train whilst a Gresley Class J19 rebuild of Hill's GER design, No. 64669 marshalls a freight train on the left. To the right stands what is believed to be an ex-Great Central Railway Class C4 Atlantic.

P. Ransome Wallis/National Railway Museum

The 'down' 1.40pm King's Cross to Peterborough stopping train, comprising a variety of stock (including two dissimilar pairs of articulated coaches to the rear) still with LNER lettering and in teak livery, on 20th March 1949, headed, however, by 'British Railways' lettered No. 61121 in partly-lined black livery as it enters the cutting north of Potters Bar at about 40 mph.

E. D. Bruton

Immingham based No. 61082 at Sleaford with an 'up' Class 'B' passenger train on 23rd June 1958.

R. C. Riley

On 15th April 1954 No. 61097 passed Brookmans Park with an 'up' Class 'B' local Hitchin to King's Cross train.

Philip J. Kelley

No. 61200 approaches Welwyn Viaduct bearing Class 'C' headcode works home to King's Cross (34A) with an 'up' empty stock train.

Philip J. Kelley

No. 61097 at Wood Green with a Class 'B' passenger train on 4th June 1958.

A. R. Goult

No. 61139 was the last of the first batch of North British built B1s. On 29th September 1956 it was photographed leaving Welwyn North Tunnel with the 12.50pm Cambridge to King's Cross Class 'B'.

Philip J. Kelley

On 29th September 1956 No. 61394 enters Welwyn North Tunnel with a 'down' express.
Philip J. Kelley

Showing signs of some abuse No. 61073 nears Marshmoor box with the 'up' 12.15pm ex-Skegness Butlins express.
Philip J. Kelley

No. 61131 passing Sudbury Hill with the 6.45am Pinxton (GN) to Marylebone special on 7th June 1952.
LCGB/Ken Nunn Collection

Wearing Class 'B' code No. 61046 nears Marshmoor box on 2nd September 1961 with an 'up' engineers train.

Philip J. Kelley

The North Eastern

No. 61084 leaves Newcastle with an express for Liverpool comprised of ex-London, Midland & Scottish stock. The exact date is not recorded but it is certainly post May 1948 for it was then that the front number plate was fitted: 'BRITISH RAILWAYS' is painted on the tender, which has that 'new paint' look. There is no shed plate but the locomotive is based at York. It is possible that this was one of the trains used to test public reaction to the proposed new livery.

Real Photographs

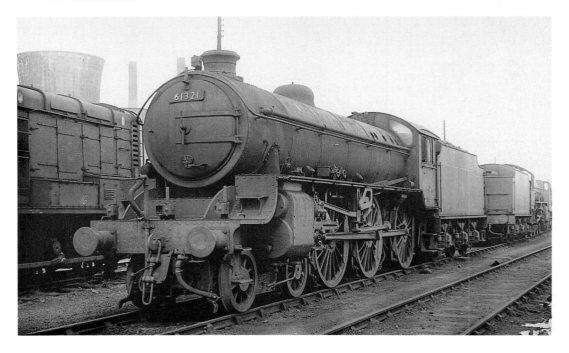

Darlington Motive Power Depot on 9th May 1964. No. 61321 is 'at home' and at rest. This picture serves well to show the fitment of the electric lamps and the footstep on the smokebox door to facilitate access to the top lampbracket.

H. R. Davies

July 3rd 1959 and No. 61322 waits at Newcastle with the 4.34pm express for Berwick. On the far side of the platform stands a train of North Tyne electric stock, with one of the new dmus on the adjacent track.

T. J. Edgington

From the second batch a Darlington built B1, No. 61031 *Reedbuck* waits to depart from York with a Railway Correspondence & Travel Society special. The locomotive was based at York and had been beautifully prepared. The arm of the law appears to be eyeing the photographer with some suspicion!

T. J. Edgington

No. 61071 received its British Railways identity in April 1948. Here, the locomotive is seen leaving York later that year with an express comprised of ex-LMS stock from Liverpool to Newcastle. 'BRITISH RAILWAYS' is inscribed upon the tender and whilst there is no shed-plate 'YORK' appears on the bufferbeam. This could also be one of the trains used to test reaction of the public to the proposed new livery.

Real Photographs

No. 61218 waits to leave York with an express on 6th July 1956.   *A. R. Goult*

No. 61039 *Steinbok* on York crossing, 16th July 1950.   *E. D. Bruton*

On 6th July 1956 No. 61053 (an Ipswich engine) manifested itself at York wearing an express headcode and hauling a six-wheeled balcony coach.

A. R. Goult

London & North Western

On the foggy morning of 7th January 1961 No. 61220 of Thornaby shed passes Farnley Junction, ex-LMS shed Leeds, with an express from Teesside for Manchester.

H. N. James

On 15th June 1956 No. 61022 *Sassaby* waits to depart from Carlisle under the LNW signals with the 9.05am to Newcastle. The leading coach is clearly in need of a little affection.

T. J. Edgington

At Carlisle Motive Power Depot on 7th March 1964 No. 61099 shunts a dead sister engine. Electrification is in evidence, for overhead wire warning signs are on the running plate.

H. R. Davies

Great Northern and London & North Western Joint

No. 61188, the last but one B1 built by Vulcan Foundry, works on to the Leicester Belgrave Road branch at Marefield Junction with the 1.30pm Skegness to Leicester express on 1st July 1961.

H. N. James

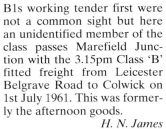

B1s working tender first were not a common sight but here an unidentified member of the class passes Marefield Junction with the 3.15pm Class 'B' fitted freight from Leicester Belgrave Road to Colwick on 1st July 1961. This was formerly the afternoon goods.

H. N. James

No. 61175 passes a sunny but overgrown Great Dalby with the 1.52pm Mablethorpe to Leicester Belgrave Road express on the same day as the previous illustration.

H. N. James

On 1st September 1962 No. 61141 passes Melton Mowbray North with a Mablethorpe to Leicester Belgrave Road express.

H. N. James

Midland and London & North Western Joint

Doncaster (36A) based No. 61360 at Cromford with the High Peak Railtour on 27th June 1964. The locomotive was the first of the final batch built by the North British Locomotive Co. Ltd.

D. B. Swale

The Lanky

Bradford Exchange on 19th May 1956. Bradford (37C) based No. 61267 waits to leave with the 8.43am express to King's Cross.

T. J. Edgington

North of the Border

Running in on the Glasgow line a Peppercorn Pacific, No. 60119 *Patrick Stirling* (running up light engine from Haymarket Motive Power Depot) occupies the 'up' 'Forth Bridge' line. B1 No. 61102 of Dundee (62B) heads through West Princes Street Gardens, Edinburgh with the 8.47am Class 'B' Inverkeithing to Edinburgh Waverley stopping train on 8th June 1951.

E. D. Bruton

No. 61025 *Pallah* from Tweedmouth Motive Power Depot (52D), probably a 'common user' engine, as it is seen at Saughton Junction, on the 'down' 3.43pm Edinburgh Waverley to Larbert Class 'B' train, on the Glasgow line at about 35 mph on 3rd July 1954.

E. D. Bruton

Just breasting the last yards of the 1 in 96 of Cockburnpath Bank to the easier 1 in 200 on to Grantshouse, St Margaret's (64A) based No. 61398 heads the 'up' 3.45pm Edinburgh Waverley to Berwick Class 'B' stopping train on Saturday 26th June 1954.

E. D. Bruton

In the brilliant evening sunshine of Wednesday 23rd June 1954 the 'down' 6.55pm Edinburgh Waverley to Perth express is leaving the west end bay Platform 4 of Waverley station. Polished but slightly dusty, No. 61341 (based at Eastfield Motive Power Depot, Glasgow) is storming away towards the Mound Tunnel – the first two coaches are in plain British Railways' red.

E. D. Bruton

On 31st May 1960 No. 61396 enters Fort William station with an express. Despite having high lamp irons at the top of the smokebox door there is no foot-step adjacent to the shedplate.

A. R. Goult

The 'down' 6.55pm express from Edinburgh Waverley to Perth via the Forth Bridge, hurries along at about 60 mph near Corstorphine as it crosses the plains west of the city. It is headed by St Margarets Motive Power Depot (64A) based No. 61330 at 7.02pm in Friday 2nd July 1954, under a stormy sky.

E. D. Bruton

The first of the Gorton built batch, No. 61340 is seen between Calton Hill Tunnel and Abbey Mill Junction, east of Edinburgh with a rake of East Coast stock in carmine and cream livery on 2nd July 1954, wearing Class 'C' code. The locomotive is Eastfield (65A) based.

E. D. Bruton

No. 61349, the last B1 built by Gorton, with a 'down' express at Inverkeithing in 1949. No trace of ownership upon the tender but the smokebox door sports the footstep normally associated with locomotives having the high-placed numberplate and lamp irons.

Real Photographs

'At home' at Dunfermline (62C) No. 61350, the first of Darlington's last batch of ten B1s, passes under the coaling tower in August 1966.

D. B. Swale

Dominated by the volcanic puy (on which stands Edinburgh Castle) a pair of B1s, Nos 61342 (from Glasgow Eastfield Motive Power Depot (65A), piloting 61134, swing round the curve in Princes Street Gardens. The train is the 'up' 5pm Glasgow to Edinburgh Waverley express. For some reason a headboard is carried reversed on the pilot locomotive.

E. D. Bruton

Soft evening sunlight illuminates the 'down' 6pm Class 'A' Edinburgh Waverley to Glasgow Queen Street as it is accelerated through Princes Street Gardens, headed by No. 61180, whilst sister locomotive No. 61244 *Strang Steel* waits 'wrong road' for the signal, on 23rd June 1954. It looks as though that road is signalled for reversible working at the cross-over as back lights are clearly seen!

E. D. Bruton

On the afternoon of 23rd June 1954 the 'up' 'Waverley Route' 2.35pm stopping train from Edinburgh Waverley to Carlisle via Hawick, by-passing the platform at Portobello station, is in charge of Darlington built No. 61356 from St Margarets Motive Power Depot, Edinburgh (64A). The mandatory oil lamp is carried above the electric headlamp for the Class 'B' headcode, but on the smokebox 'iron' instead of in front of the chimney – a short fireman perhaps? The top lamp iron is long enough for both lamps!

E. D. Bruton

On the West Highland main line near Inverlochy the 'down' 5.30am Glasgow Queen Street to Fort William and Mallaig 'express' loaded to eight coaches, including one or more from the overnight "Aberdonian" from London King's Cross, is double headed on 19th June 1951. The train engine, Gresley Class K2/2 No. 61791 *Loch Laggan* is piloted by Gorton built 'BRITISH RAILWAYS' lettered B1 No. 61344 from Glasgow, Eastfield (65A). Steam has been shut off both engines as Mallaig Junction is not far ahead – they are dropping down the bank at about 40 mph.

E. D. Bruton

On ex-Glasgow & South Western Railway territory No. 61243 *Sir Harold Mitchell* was photographed at Ayr shed on 30th July 1965.

H. R. Davies

Another view of the 'down' 5.30pm Glasgow Queen Street to Fort William and Mallaig, this time in June 1951 at Mallaig Junction. The ten-coach train, conveying sleeping cars from the overnight "Aberdonian" from King's Cross, is headed by Gresley Class K2/2 2-6-0 No. 61781 *Loch Morrar* piloted by B1 No. 61344. The Mallaig extension line swings away to the left behind the B1 and a glimpse is caught of the extension sidings, mainly used for the storage of fish vans until called to Mallaig for loading. Note the ex-North British Railway lattice-post signal fitted with an upper quadrant arm.

E. D. Bruton

An 'up' Royal Navy Leave Special, under Class 'A' head-code, is hustled through North Queensferry Tunnel on 8th June 1951 by No. 61403 from the final batch of B1s built at Darlington. The locomotive is fitted with extended lamp irons but without the associated electric headlamps.

E. D. Bruton

An idyllic picture as No. 61197 heads a Class 'A' express freight along the West Highland line near Tyndrum in 1959.

P. Ramsome-Wallis/National Railway Museum

'At home' at Dundee Tay Bridge (62B) an ex-North British Railways shed, Vulcan Foundry built No. 61180 rests with sister engine No. 61102.

H. R. Davies

On former Caledonian Railway territory No. 61330 from Carstairs Motive Power Depot (64D), enters Motherwell with an 'up' Class 'F' express freight. The date is 8th July 1955.

T. J. Edgington

Nearly 2½ years into Nationalisation, on 29th May 1950, Gorton built No. 61348 still bears 'BRITISH RAILWAYS' upon the tender and the coaches remain in teak livery. As the locomotive was only built in June 1949 it is unlikely to have been called to works simply to have the tender repainted. The Kittybrewster (61A) based locomotive is seen at Craigellachie.

A. R. Goult

Sunshine and shadow at Edinburgh Waverley station on 28th July 1961. No. 61308 has not ventured far from home, having been built by North British Locomotive Co. Ltd. (Strange things seem to have happened to the bottom of the smokebox door.)

H. G. Davies

The Great Western

Whisper it low! B1s even found their way onto hallowed Great Western Railway metals. On 6th October 1951 No. 61175 waits at Kensington Olympia at the head of a Stephenson Locomotive Society special before the start of the "London Junction Railtour". The train is composed of a ten-coach set of ex-Great Western centre corridor stock from Old Oak Common.

E. D. Bruton

Banbury on 24th August 1956 as No. 61192 passes with a York to Swansea express. It is not beyond the realms of possibility that the scene will one day be repeated – other than for the cattle wagons on the right.

T. J. Edgington

Apparently still in London & North Eastern Railway apple green livery, but with the British Railways' number painted on the bufferbeam, No. 61251 *Oliver Bury* was photographed near Yatton with the 10.40am Penzance to Birmingham express on 7th July 1948. The locomotive performed particularly well on the London, Midland Region during the Locomotive Exchanges.

LCGB/Ken Nunn Collection

On 15th July 1950 No. 61063 of Annesley (38B) passes an ex-GWR pannier tank whilst on its way through High Wycombe, with a Ramsgate to Nottingham through working via Kensington Olympia.

H. N. James

No. 61315 leaves Swindon with the 10.55am Swansea to Sheffield Victoria on 9th August 1953.

LCGB/Ken Nunn Collection

On Southern Metals

The last of the first batch of B1s built by the North British Locomotive Co. Ltd, No. 61139 passes Polegate (ex-LBSCR) with a Hitchin to Eastbourne excursion on 15th June 1952. The stock is a nicely mixed set!

S. C. Nash

On 24th May 1953 No. 61273 leaves Patcham Tunnel on a return Brighton to Leicester excursion under Class 'C' headcode. But this is the Southern Region, where different rules applied. The engine is on a Stewarts Lane duty, working to Clapham Junction via Tulse Hill and Brixton.

S. C. Nash

No. 61138 on ex-South Eastern & Chatham Railway territory with the 10.35am Victoria to Ramsgate, near Broadstairs. It is 25th May 1953. The train is diverting onto the 1926 deviation and the formation of the old Ramsgate Harbour line is on the right.

S. C. Nash

No. 61015 *Duiker* at Herne Bay in 1953. The appearance of B1s on the Southern Region in that year was occasioned by a locomotive shortage caused by the failure of a crank axle on one of the Bulleid Pacifics and the need for all these locomotives to be checked and rectified.

P. Ransome-Wallis/National Railway Museum

North British built No. 61133 enters Margate with the 3.20pm Ramsgate to Victoria on 25th May 1953. It is interesting that 'BRITISH RAILWAYS' is still inscribed upon the tender so late in time, indicting infrequent visits to works.

S. C. Nash

Annesley (38B) based No. 61063 leaves Kensington Olympia with the 12.10pm Ramsgate to Sheffield on 25th July 1953.

S. C. Nash

On ex-London, Brighton & South Coast lines No. 61329 leaves Littlehampton with a return excursion to Chingford on 25th May 1957. The second coach is still in teak finish.

S. C. Nash

Cambridge (31A) based No. 61203 near Farnborough North with a Cambridge to North Camp special for the Farnborough Air Show on 7th September 1958.

S. C. Nash

Preservation

Released from the North British Locomotive's works in November 1947, bearing the builder's number 26165, No. 1264 had been built at a contract price of £14,985. The locomotive was despatched to Stratford for painting and acceptance trials and from thence to Parkeston where it entered service in the December. As number 61264 the engine was displaced by 'modernisation' for the Great Eastern section was one of the first to be dieselized and it was transferred to Colwick in December 1960. In July 1965 she was photographed at Bestwood (GN) with an 'up' coal train.

D. B. Swale

Four months later the locomotive was withdrawn, but instead of being sent for scrap was retained for carriage heating duties as Departmental No. 29, continuing to work at Colwick. There she became very run down, to the point of losing the centre driving wheels. When final withdrawal came in 1967 the driving wheels were replaced and the engine sold as scrap to Woodham Bros of Barry, whence she arrived in April 1968 – the only ex-LNER locomotive ever to go to the South Wales scrapyard. No. 61264 lay derelict at Barry until 1973 when a group of enthusiasts from North London visited the yard with a view to buying a locomotive for preservation. Following two inspections the B1 was declared to be reasonably sound, and with the aid of a loan, the purchase was made in 1974. Now the property of the Thompson B1 Locomotive Trust Ltd No. 61264 left Barry late on the afternoon of 20th July 1976.

E. Drummond Reynolds

The following day the two low loaders from Leicester Heavy Haulage were photographed heading north along the M5 motorway. Rarely can a B1's tender have followed so far behind the locomotive!

E. Drummond Reynolds

Thirteen years after arrival on the Great Central Railway the frames and wheels of No. 61264 were re-united in March 1989, and the first major steps on the road of the rebuild had been taken. The locomotive's owners have met and are overcoming some major problems with the boiler. Rebuilding this item alone will have cost about four times as much as the engine did when new. The aim is main line running and British Rail's inspectors are being consulted every step of the way.

Anthony V. Gregory

No. 61306 was one of the last three B1s in service, its last day in traffic being 30th September 1967 when it hauled the last steam hauled portion of the "Yorkshire Pullman". Acquired by Gerald Boden shortly thereafter she was named *Mayflower* and restored in LNER apple green livery. Based for some time at Carnforth, from whence she worked on the main line, No. 61306 was photographed on the turntable wearing LNER livery and a BR smokebox numberplate. 'Carnforth' is inscribed on the bufferbeam.

T. J. Edgington

Following the stint at Carnforth No. 1306 moved to the Great Central Railway at Loughborough. On 27th September 1986 the locomotive leaves Loughborough with the 17.15 for Rothley, fittingly bearing "The Mayflower" headboard. On the bufferbeam 'Carnforth' has given way to 'Annesley'.

Dr W. A. Sharman

Strange shedmates. A scene which might have occurred in working days, but somewhat unlikely. At a Birmingham Railway Museum gala day *Mayflower* stands beside ex-GWR pannier tank No. 7752 on 9th June 1985.

G. Wignall

A more likely combination. No. 1306 and the Gresley Society's N2 class 0-6-2T, No. 4744 at Quorn on the Great Central Railway.

G. Wignall

Almost a re-enactment of the scene on page 62 No. 1306 and the National Railway Museum's ex-Great Central Class D11/1 4-4-0 No. 506 *Butler-Henderson* work tender first to Loughborough.

G. Wignall

November 13th 1988 and No. 1306 leaves Loughborough with the 13.00 for Rothley. The bufferbeam now reads 'Hull' – a presage of things to come.

Dr W. A. Sharman

A nice side-on shot of *Mayflower* leaving Loughborough for Quorn.   *G. Wignall*

Autumn draws on as No. 1306 leaves Rothley with the 15.05 for Loughborough.   *Dr W. A. Sharman*

On 2nd October 1988 *Mayflower* crosses Swithland Reservoir with the 11.45 from Loughborough to Rothley.
Dr W. A. Sharman